Culinary Adventures in Marrakech

Penguin Books

peta mathias

Culinary Adventures in Marrakech

PENGUIN BOOKS
Published by the Penguin Group
Penguin Group (NZ), 67 Apollo Drive, Rosedale,
North Shore 0632, New Zealand (a division of Pearson New Zealand Ltd)
Penguin Group (USA) Inc., 375 Hudson Street,
New York, New York 10014, USA
Penguin Group (Canada), 90 Eglinton Avenue East, Suite 700, Toronto,
Ontario, M4P 2Y3, Canada (a division of Pearson Penguin Canada Inc.)
Penguin Books Ltd, 80 Strand, London, WC2R 0RL, England
Penguin Ireland, 25 St Stephen's Green,
Dublin 2, Ireland (a division of Penguin Books Ltd)
Penguin Group (Australia), 250 Camberwell Road, Camberwell,
Victoria 3124, Australia (a division of Pearson Australia Group Pty Ltd)
Penguin Books India Pvt Ltd, 11, Community Centre,
Panchsheel Park, New Delhi – 110 017, India
Penguin Books (South Africa) (Pty) Ltd, 24 Sturdee Avenue,
Rosebank, Johannesburg 2196, South Africa

Penguin Books Ltd, Registered Offices: 80 Strand, London, WC2R 0RL, England

First published by Penguin Group (NZ), 2010
1 3 5 7 9 10 8 6 4 2

Copyright © Peta Mathias, 2010
Copyright images © as per page 276

The right of Peta Mathias to be identified as the author of this work in terms of
section 96 of the Copyright Act 1994 is hereby asserted.

Publisher Alison Brook
Project Editor Kate Stockman

Designed and typeset by Sara Bellamy
Prepress by Image Centre Ltd
Printed in China by South China Printing Company

ISBN 9780143204596

A catalogue record for this book is available
from the National Library of New Zealand.

www.penguin.co.nz

Thanks to:

Jeff and Jane Avery of Red Head Media Group, for making the series and being intrepid and fearless. To David Horsman of Fête Accomplie Culinary Trips, thank you for the wonderful photos and extraordinary talent with a gin and tonic. To Florence Verley of Dar Tasmayoun, thank you for your hospitality and for thinking we're interesting. Thank you to the gastronomads, Errol and Rona Chave, Joan Browning, Jeanne Highland and Jan McNee. Finally, to Adriano Pirani of Hôtel du Trésor, thanks for your hospitality and a great Italian accent!

Contents

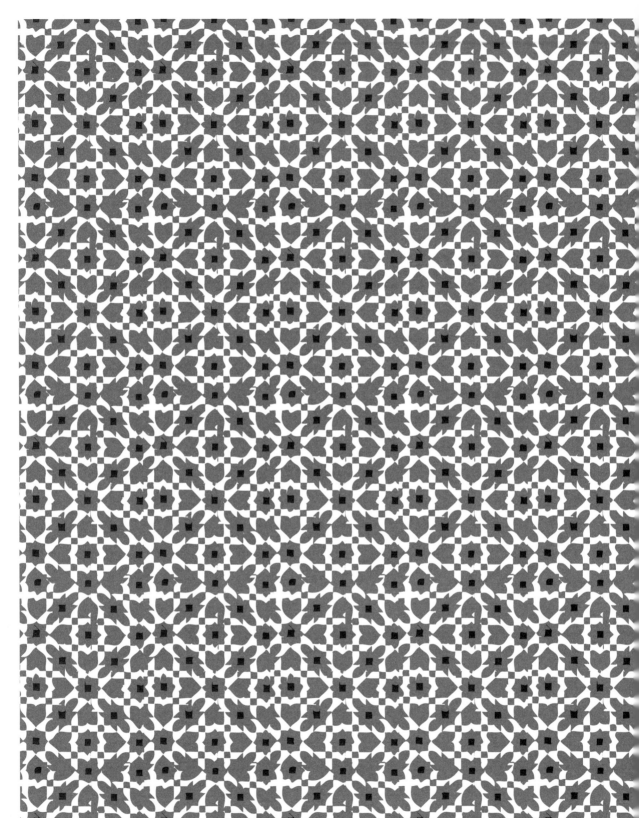

Introduction

The first thing you hear when you set foot on
Moroccan soil is: Allahu akbar, Allahu *akbar, Ashhadu
an la Ilah ila Allah, Ashhadu an Mohammedan
rasul Allah, Haya ala as-sala, Haya ala assala.*

There is no God but Allah, and Mohammed is His Prophet. The
muezzins chant from the minarets of mosques five times a day.
Loud speakers amplify the call to make sure you get the message.
This is the defining sound of Morocco – it confirms you are in a
foreign country, a land of ritual and tradition, and lets you know
that everything is going to be madly exotic.

In her bible on Moroccan cookery, *Couscous and Other Good
Food from Morocco*, Paula Wolfert says four things are necessary
for a truly great cuisine, and Morocco has them all. First, there
must be an abundance of ingredients in a rich land. Second, a
variety of cultural influences need to be at play. Third, the country
should be a great civilisation – it should have had its time in the
sun. And fourth, a refined palace with the demands of a cultivated
court is needed to challenge the nation's cooks. Royalty and
money require that a cuisine reaches great heights. What makes the
cuisine of Morocco so good is its imperial past – a past of heroic
exploits, sophisticated culture and great civilisation.

In a culture of luxury, cooks must fly to the limits of their creative abilities. Morocco has a clear culture of food and Moroccans see the world in quite a different set of colours before a good meal than they do after. Not all countries are like this. Not all countries breathe and celebrate their food as an integral part of their culture. Traditional dishes are the product of collective genius. No individual Moroccan invents a dish; dishes are invented by everyone, owned by everyone and can't be reinvented.

To understand the importance of Moroccan food, you need to delve into the country's history and changing cultural make-up. Northern Moroccans, whose second language is Spanish, can be quite light skinned with pale eyes. Southern Moroccans, or Sahraoui, can be almost black because they come from the Sahara. In Marrakech, the second language is French. My friend's mother had an Andalusian grandmother from Chefchaouen. This shows in her black eyes, eyebrows and lashes, round face and maiden name of Serag. She wears lots of kohl on her eyes and dyes her hair very black. She makes paella, which is common in the north.

The gracious, beautifully spoken Mr Sefrioni, who owns the luxury hotel Riad Fès in Fès, waxed lyrical about Moroccan history and Fassi food. He told me a long story to explain why he had pale skin and blue eyes; a story that went right back to the eighth century. He said there are no pure Berbers or Arabs in Morocco because the country has experienced so many invasions and waves of immigration. They are Berber with a suspected Nordic strain, Phoenician, Roman, Vandal, Byzantine, Arab, Portuguese, Spanish, French. This mad mix of cultures and people is responsible for the sensuous and unusual cuisine: tagines and harira soups come from the Berbers; the Moors brought olive oil, almonds, herbs and fruits; the Bedouins contributed dates, grains, bread and milk; and the Arabs, who learned culinary secrets from the Persians, brought with them spices from India. Fès, now Morocco's third largest city, was the Athens of North Africa, advanced in astronomy, theology, mathematics, medicine and metallurgy when Europe was in the quagmire of the Middle Ages.

The Moroccan Moors were Muslims of Berber and Arab descent who took over North Africa, Spain and parts of Portugal from the eighth century. In Spain you notice all the sugar, almonds and oranges in the pastries. These ingredients come from the ancient Arabs. The marzipan sweets filled with sugared egg threads and almonds are obviously Moroccan, as is their most well-known paste made from figs, almonds, cocoa, cinnamon and lemon rind. Spanish and Portuguese can thank the Arabs for their land rich in almond, carob, olive, fig and navel orange trees. The Moroccan Moors stayed in Évora, Portugal, from AD 711 to AD 1165. The city had a mosque, a castle and irrigated land producing wheat, fruit and vegetables. Three centuries later, their influence was still felt in Moorish quarters and gardens were hung with striped Moroccan rugs. Today, the pastries are still full of honey, pine nuts, orange water and almonds.

Arab Andalusia was absolutely fabulous – rich, powerful and a centre for learning, artistry, fashion, gastronomy and social graces. At a time when feudal Europe was still scratching its bum with a stick, Moorish Spain had brilliant metropolises complete with libraries, street lighting, sophisticated public gardens and amphitheatres. Córdoba was described by travellers as a mythic fairy tale land with its international trade markets, schools, mosques and ordered suburbs. Now this will tell you how refined the Moors were: in the mosque Mezquita, which is now a Catholic cathedral, trees were planted in the courtyard to extend outwards from the rows of columns inside the building. The stupendous architecture of the massive mosque had one side completely open, which allowed the light to stream in. The Moors designed the mosque to not only be beautiful, with its endless rows of columns and red-and-white striped arches, but also to be open and therefore free the mind. Time went by in Andalusia, and the Muslims and Christians who had always got along so well stopped doing so. By the seventeenth century, thanks in large part to the Christian King Fernando and Queen Isabella, the destruction of fabulous Andalusia was complete.

Queen Isabella threw out the Jews at the same time as she did the Moors, and they all sailed across the water to Morocco, taking their great cuisine with them. The Jews, however, have a much more ancient history in Morocco, dating right back to the first century. Although the Jewish population of Morocco is relatively small, their gastronomic influence over the whole country is enormous. It is said that fully half the recipes in Morocco are of Jewish origin. In the Middle Ages, Jews were living in Mogador (now Essaouira) under royal protection and were responsible for much of its prosperity. Their influence is still obvious in the mellahs (Jewish markets), where the goods you can buy include briouat (triangle pastry filled with fish) and a slow-cooked stew of beef, tongue and feet, which is called dafina and normally cooked on Friday for the Saturday Sabbath. Jewish cooks also invented the justly feared rate farci – stuffed lamb spleen. They used orange juice and flowers for perfume, medicine, honey and aromatherapy. Today, Moroccan Muslims and Jews live side by side in harmony, sharing their traditions and culinary history, and the best food market in Marrakech is still in the mellah.

There are two strata of food in Morocco: that eaten by the ordinary people and that enjoyed by the aristocracy, which experts consider far superior. I'm not so sure there is a huge difference in essence: a tagine tastes more or less the same and is made with the same cuts of meat in the souk as it is in the palace; warka pastry is just that whether you're sitting on a mud floor or a silk banquette. The blessing of Moroccan culture is that the poorest shoe merchant will make himself a sensual, colourful feast of fish tagine with lentils and vegetables for his lunch; whereas a poor Englishman will have a revolting meat pie. And country ways die hard in Morocco: every family seems to feel they have to own a sheep or a cow. You'd have to be grievously poor not to. Moroccans spend more money feeding their animals than they do feeding themselves – but this is not out of love. It is so they can eat the beast when the time of Aïd el Kebhir arrives – the festival of the sacrifice of the lamb which comes fifty days after Ramadan. They keep the animals in apartments, in gardens, on the roof, in sheds, anywhere they can. I heard of a man whose only way of getting his ailing mother down from the mountains to live in town under his care was to let her bring her cow with her and keep it on the roof of his apartment building.

In the ten years I lived in Paris during the 1980s, I could often be found slurping down tagines and couscous stews, both with North African friends in their kitchens and in the many restaurants I visited. I loved this food because it was very aromatic, served in an unusual way, and you were allowed to eat it with your hands. My friends and I would go to the mosque in the 5th arrondissement and have a feast in the restaurant after lying around in the hammam (bath house), lethargic with hedonism. We'd wander back through the tearooms after leaving the hammam, meaning to exit but we never did. Ever. We always intended to keep walking but the dark, almond-eyed waiter doing the rounds with mint tea and sweet pastries always caught our eyes and we would soon find ourselves reclining on one of the Moorish embroidered banquettes. Just for ten minutes. Well okay, actually the whole afternoon would go by as we got into involved discussions with other patrons, and before you could say harissa (chilli paste) it was dark outside and we were hungry. Fortunately, the mosque provided for all eventualities. We would walk through a side door to find ourselves in a sumptuous Algerian-style dining room. It was not the best couscous in Paris but I could have eaten a horse after the exhaustions of the hammam.

We would gather up new-found acquaintances and move into the dining room to order lamb couscous with spicy merguez (sausage) on the side. The waiter gave us large soup plates, which were carefully wiped with a white cloth before our very eyes. Then a huge platter of meat arrived at the table followed by a golden plate of semolina, hand rolled and steamed over stock. Next came the vegetables swimming in a deep bowl of perfumed broth – courgettes, chick peas, potatoes, carrots, raisins and sweet baby turnips. We all spooned lots of couscous into the middle of our plates on top of which we piled vegetables and broth. We passed the meat around and placed it on the side of our plates. Finally, the harissa, mixed in with a bit of broth, was poured over the lot. This is the Algerian style of serving couscous; in Morocco it is served as one composite dish. We drank lots of rich red Algerian wine and kept helping ourselves until it was all gone.

Skipping forward from that time to 2001, my interest in North African, Spanish and Portuguese cooking and music prompted me to write a book on the differences, similarities and connections between these cultures, especially in regard to singing, music and food. This meant I finally got to Morocco, which was something I had been longing for all the time I had lived in Paris. I called this book *Sirocco*, after the hot, oppressive and often dusty spring and autumn wind that blows in North Africa, Syria and which eventually reaches Europe.

My interest in Morocco and its cuisine held steady and in 2007 I decided to expand my Fête Accomplie Culinary Adventures, which I run with my business partner David Horsman, by adding Marrakech as a destination. Needless to say, this meant at least three indulgent recce trips to set things up. Here's the low-down on Marrakech: lush, affluent, Euro-influenced chic, outrageously exotic nightclubs, designer kaftans, tagines, crab sushi, sexy North African cool and drop-dead stylish accommodation. Forget hashish, backpacks, dodgy carpets and 3000 ways to do couscous – Marrakech has hit the big time. You can get a perfectly acceptable tagine in a Berber joint for 35 dirhams and you can get almost the same thing in the most expensive and fabulous restaurant in Marrakech, Dar Yacout. It's all part of the charismatic culinary experience of the place. When not out researching, I sat on my bed at Hôtel du Trésor in the medina sipping mint tea and eating pomegranates and chocolates.

If you want to go to a contemporary French/Moroccan bistro, go to Un Déjeuner à Marrakech in the souk. If you want the best traditional cuisine go to Al Fassia, which is entirely run by women. If you want the best sardine kefta tagine, go to a tiny hole-in-the-wall restaurant with no name in Place Kedima in the souk. Ask for Amina when you get there. From another Amina, the cook at Hôtel du Trésor, I learned an intense, unusual way of cooking eggplant – a Moroccan way to turn eggplant into heaven. Moroccans call all starters salad, whether hot or cold, and Amina's heavenly eggplant dish, zaahlouk, is served at room temperature. They like mixing textures and the different way food feels in their mouths. Bsaha!

There is something decadent about sweating around the souks, arguing with taxi drivers, getting covered in dust, then returning to quiet, ordered comfort behind a little unassuming door. Of course, this is how people stay sane in the medina – huge houses are hidden down dim alleyways and everything is protected by very high walls. Medina homes are not built to show off to the neighbours – they are built to provide privacy and tranquillity.

I wake up in the morning and throw the shutters open. It's dawn and the first prayers of the day have just hurled over the rooftops of Marrakech. The second thing you hear after prayers is birds singing and kissing each other. All internal gardens are built to attract different birds, produce scents, provide a variety of fruit and flowers and to please the ears with tinkling fountains. Breakfast is home-made jam, honey, tea, freshly squeezed orange juice and a basketful of freshly baked, still-warm breads – m'lawi, flat bread, pancake and croissant. If you are staying in a Moroccan household, you will also be offered these things for afternoon tea or le goûter.

Later in the day I am lying on a slab in the hammam exactly the way God made me, indulging in one of my favourite pastimes of steam room, scrub and massage. In between being rubbed with clay, having the top layer of my skin scrubbed off, enjoying buckets of water poured over my head and being sprinkled with rosewater, I hear the life story of my beautiful masseuse, Fátima. Married off at nineteen to a cousin who turned out to be a dud, within four months she was home again. After I had heard about the divorce, we quickly moved on to food and by the time I was having oil rubbed through my hair, I had been invited to her place for dinner. That's how it goes in these exotic places. There's the opportunity to cut through all preliminaries with a stranger and communicate what is important: family, food and friendship. If the taxi driver in some madly exciting place like Vietnam, Rajasthan or Morocco invites you to his mother's home for dinner, say yes, because that is the best food you will eat. These particular countries have very sophisticated, developed cuisines and the locals absolutely adore it when you show interest in and knowledge about their food.

It's hot, hot, hot and busy, busy, busy. Marrakechi hate going to bed and seem to do most of their business at night. David and I set off to visit Dar Tasmayoun, the country residence our clients will stay in. As with everything in Morocco, nothing goes according to plan. In fact, the only plan to have in Morocco is no plan. If you have any remote attachment to order, control or direction you would have to rip people's throats out with your teeth. It doesn't matter what time you get anywhere because time passes on slippered feet; in fact, time is a valueless commodity. Morocco is at once a place left behind by time and a place which no longer exists – their centuries-old lifestyles live alongside modernity and technology. For example, Moroccans are in love with cellphones because they are more reliable than landlines and cover a much wider territory. I even saw peasants on donkeys talking on cellphones. The Moroccan love of cellphones may have some influence on their not understanding the concept of planning in advance – they make plans on the hoof.

When you say, 'I want to confirm with you that you will come and play music at my house on Tuesday in two weeks' time,' they ask 'Why? Call us in two weeks.' So we turn up at the country house with our complicated, detailed schedule that we'd sent the French owner, Florence, months earlier. She says she never received it and has a heart attack when we show it to her. After a few glasses of rosé we all love each other in the nicest possible way. The lady Berber musicians are now coming on another night because they found something else to do on the night they had confirmed with us, and they don't have transport so we have to go get them. Reports have it they drink like fish (whisky out of tea cups). When I meet them they turn out to be a percussion group of various tambours and one lady with gold teeth in her brilliantly black face plays an enamel plate with castanets.

Moroccans are friendly and hospitable but life is very full on and practically medieval in places. Just when you decide you don't want to go native after all and if you see another snake charmer you might scream, you discover mountains of rosebuds, pyramids of pomegranates and dozens of birds chirping in the orange trees. On one of our recce trips we fell right into the middle of the religious purification fast of Ramadan. If you think Moroccans are elusive and difficult to deal with on a good day, try hungry, thirsty, nicotine-deprived, sex-starved Moroccans. Ramadan falls in the ninth month of the Islamic calendar and the timing changes every year. A strict fast is adhered to for thirty days, which means no eating, no drinking, no smoking and no sex from dawn to dusk. This fast is enforced by law: if you're caught breaking it in public, woe betide you. But what actually happens, from what I saw, is that they drink, eat and fornicate all night. They don't get enough sleep and are grouchy all day. On the last day of Ramadan, which is called Eid ul-Fitr, everyone goes completely berserk and it's not a good idea for you to be on the streets. The naughty ones get roaring drunk; the regular ones celebrate wildly in an orgy of eating, smoking, spending and present giving; the good ones give to the poor and hand pastries out all over town. The upside of our research is that Adriano Pirani, the dapper, charming Italian designer who owns Hôtel du Trésor, which is where our clients will stay in the medina, reveals himself to be a fabulous partner-in-crime. This guy knows how to organise a party, decorate a salon and steal a scene. He can also find the most handsome waiters in Marrakech.

In the meantime, with partners Jane and Jeff Avery, I set up my own television production company, Red Head Media Group, to make food/travel television shows. I had been presenting similar shows for TVNZ for twelve years: *Taste NZ, Taste Takes Off, Toast NZ* and *A Taste of Home*, but TVNZ chose to stop making these prime-time, top-rating shows. Jeff was so incensed when I told him this he said, 'Right, from now on we will make our own shows, you will be unplugged from the structured TVNZ way of filming, and you will make television exactly the way you want.' It took me a while to adjust to this. When shooting, I would ask Jeff and Jane questions like, 'Is it okay if I wear this necklace? Do you think saying "bloody buggery" is too straightforward? Shall I take my rings off while cooking?' The very calm, relaxed Jeff's answer was always the same: 'Guess what, Peta? You're now the boss and you can do anything you want. Could you just give those broad beans another stir please and I'll do the close-up.' Male camera people and directors don't care what you look like – you could have lipstick going up your nose and they wouldn't notice – so having Jane directing was great because she would say 'posture' and I would put my shoulders down. We started off our new partnership with a straight cooking DVD and with the confidence that only comes from having done too many non-prescription drugs in your youth, we decided our second project would be to film the progress of my clients' culinary experience in Marrakech and turn it into a six-part television series.

We wrote out a loose proposal of how we thought things would proceed, bought some plane tickets and leapt over the safety barriers of our ordered lives. Jane decided to structure the series and segments around food groups and places: pastilla, tangia, mechoui, spices, olives, couscous, tagine, trid, bread, pastries, sardines, souk, mint tea, herbs, salads, argan oil, Place Djemaa el Fna and so on. When the time came, David and I were already in Marrakech sipping mint tea and whipping all our contacts into a frenzy of obedience. Jane and Jeff arrived at night after a twenty-four-hour flight from New Zealand. They looked like dead fish and were hauling large amounts of film equipment, folders bursting with permission-to-film letters from the Moroccan Ministry of Culture and bags full of anti-emetics. I ordered in a tagine for them and said goodnight. Believe it or not, the next morning, suffering from jet lag, no ability to speak the lingo and no knowledge of the medina, they strapped their equipment on and marched out into the field. Talk about intrepid – they proceeded to shoot the six-part television series in two weeks. That's a task that would take a normal film crew two months.

Jeff was shooting and Jane producing and directing, which mostly consisted of saying, 'Peta, stop eating. I need you to do a piece-to-camera', dealing with the spontaneous combustion that is Marrakech, and managing police and anyone else who felt like accessing their inner control freak. Some television colleagues had suggested we just take small digital cameras and film under the radar, pretending we were tourists. Thank God we didn't. Thank God we had the official papers as everywhere we went we were challenged. In Safi we actually ended up in the police station, where the guide advised me to get the commissioner on his own as he would respond much more positively to a charming woman!

It turns out that Moroccans are natural television stars – relaxed, confident and happy to speak to the camera whenever asked. Nobody said no to anything; everybody thought filming a six-part series in two weeks was an excellent idea and the adorable Adriano completely pulled out all the stops for my clients. Every day he came up with something more fantastic than the day before – providing rose-perfumed water in which to wash our hands, fresh flowers in the rooms, extra special breakfasts, fabulous parties, cocktails for all of Africa, always delivered with his professional charm. Florence at Dar Tasmayoun took a huge leap of faith with us, having no experience whatsoever with organised tours, television crews or that particular type of fun which comes with New Zealanders and Australians – instant friendship, unprecedented consumption of gin and tonic and wild enthusiasm for every tiny thing. Her enthusiastic property manager, Mohamed, and humble cook, Radiga, turned into the main talent overnight. The beauty and tranquillity of Florence's house deeply affected everyone.

Once we had all the footage, the really hard work of editing began: the process of turning it all into a good story. Jeff and Jane have their own editing studio so it was all done in the basement of their home. The music we had recorded in Marrakech had to be laid down, graphics done, voice-overs recorded, promo put together and a name for the series decided upon. *Peta Unplugged in Marrakech* was born. I was back in France by the time voice-overs had to be done so I recorded them in a studio in the middle of nowhere in the South of France and sent them back to New Zealand via the internet. Then we had to find someone to buy it. We had funded it ourselves, which gave us complete control. Jeff and Jane finished two episodes, designed a wonderful blue and red title card, drew up a letter of introduction, put them all in my hot little hand and I flew to London to conquer the world and find an international distributor. We had been given some good distribution company contacts by colleagues and I visited them all, putting on my best dress and shiniest lipstick. Jane did a deal with Prime TV in New Zealand and in London I did a deal with TVF Media. This book is the story of the whole exciting process.

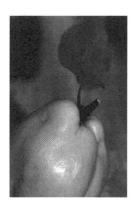

Moroccans say they are born already crying for their local dishes. Think about it – when you are lonely or sick or travelling, comfort food is what you think of first. Immigrants to another country may lose their language, national dress and the religion of their homeland. But the things that never leave are their culinary knowledge and skills. Your gastronomic past is something that is carried in the heart, the brain and the fingertips. Moroccan is a powerful cuisine: capable of healing, stimulating, warming and captivating with its carnival of salty, spicy, sweet and piquant flavours and smells. It also takes time to make and taking the time to do something properly is an art. He who has no time is dead. Moroccan cooking is generous, voluptuous, doesn't require unusual ingredients and somehow manages to be mysterious and sexy. In a galaxy of bland globalisation, traditional Moroccan dishes are a shining star of beauty and hope.

Note: Arabic words are translated phonetically so there are several different spellings for the same word. I have given the most common translations. An example is the word for pigeon pie. It is just as often spelled pastilla as bastilla as b'steeya as bistayla. There are also many variations in place names.

Chapter One Pastilla

'Have you got the welcome pastries?' *'Yep.'*
'Have you got the water?' *'Yep.'*
'Have you got the wet wipes?'
'You know I have. Do stop fussing.'

This is a conversation my business partner David and I had
numerous times as we picked up our clients, who all arrived at
Marrakech airport separately. People seem to slip into a parallel
universe when they travel, especially to challenging places. They
become disoriented and worry about tiny things; to have someone
there at the airport with a big sign saying Fête Accomplie Cooking
School, a big smile and a box of lollies is always appreciated. I
am usually the one fretting at the hotel while David rides out to
the airport to take on the role of greeter. I think I would be too
terrifying – I would rush up to exhausted strangers, throw my arms
around them and scream, 'How FABULOUS to see you.' David is
tall, handsome and languid. He greets them with, 'Good afternoon.
Lovely to meet you. Please follow my chauffeur.' The week-long
culinary experience we had planned for our clients was set in two
locations – half in the bled or countryside outside Marrakech
and half in the medina or old part of the city. We drove the forty-
five minutes straight from the airport to our country retreat, Dar
Tasmayoun guest house, which is near Ait Ourir on the route to
Ouarzazate.

 But first, let me introduce you to Marrakech. The thing that strikes you as you ride in your 'petit taxi' from the station to the hotel is how luscious and affluent Marrakech looks – this is a city with moolah. The buildings are tremendous and impressive and luxury hotels line the sweeping avenues. Marrakech completely rocks! This magnetic city has welcomed waylaid travellers for centuries. It was settled by the Muslim Almoravid leader Yusuf ibn Tashfin, who built the new city of Marrakech near the original Berber city of Aghmāt, which was bursting at the seams. He brought in craftsmen from Córdoba in Andalusia to build the most beautiful city, using the red clay that was found all around them. They built palaces, hammams, irrigated gardens, libraries, monuments and mosques. Sadly, it only lasted a century. In 1147 the Almohads conquered Marrakech, almost wrecking it in the process. They built the city again and it enjoyed great prosperity, but when the leader Ahmed el-Mansour died, it fell into decline. Because of its location halfway between the Atlantic coast and the Sahara, Marrakech was never going to stay down for long. It soon profited from the trade route – slaves, gold and ivory. In fact, it was called the golden city. Then the Saadian dynasty, which built the famous El Badi Palace, took over, followed by the Alaouites. In the twentieth century, Marrakech was famous for its sulphurous, blood-thirsty ruler: the unimaginably rich T'hami El Glaoui, last pasha of Marrakech. He was a Berber, known both for his fabulous aesthetic sense and his cruelty. When independence from the French came in 1956, it signalled the end of him and the terrible pashas.

The present king, Mohammed VI, is quite modern, not as violent as his father and is encouraging of huge renovations all over the city. Now Marrakech is mostly famous as the capital of the South and a tourist town. People travel there seeking exoticism and inspiration – this most African of Moroccan cities is a place of sweet rosebuds and honeyed dates, pungent olives, aromatic spices, dust and heat. Its colourful history is intoxicating to visitors. As a more liberal Muslim country, tradition sits comfortably alongside modern excess and, like the red clay that the city's built from, the centuries-old fascination with Marrakech never seems to fade. The centre of old Marrakech, with its ancient medina wall and Koutoubia Mosque, is truly the city's heart. These city walls, which were originally constructed of rammed earth around AD 1062, stretch for sixteen kilometres and have numerous gates, many of which are still in use.

The famous Djemaa el Fna Square is one of the busiest town squares on the planet and the frenetic, electric hubbub captivates me time and time again. The first time I came here it beckoned me like an inscrutable circus. I decided to take my digestive system in my hands and eat at a recommended food stall run by a certain Rachida. This square is colossal and the only thing that prevents you from thinking it's a giant football field with food for tourists is the fact that there are hundreds of Moroccans having a ball slurping up boiled sheep's heads, which they slice crosswise and leave open for everyone to admire. The meat is removed, sliced and served on little plates and all is devoured except the eyes. Moroccans love this place and they all crowd there in their thousands every. It is their social life – a cheap gourmet paradise of piping hot snails and ignoble bits of innards, entertainment, counselling and musical appreciation.

Why would you go to a psychologist when you can avail yourself of a snake charmer, storyteller, palm reader, astrologer or herbalist for a fraction of the price? The herbalist will cure you of your impotency, the palm reader will tell you that you will have many healthy children, but in my opinion the storyteller is the best. I cannot count the times I watched people's enraptured faces as they listened, squatting on their haunches, to the parable-like stories. Most of these people can't read or write so the storyteller teaches and clarifies life's problems and recounts the ancient tales. They are wonderfully expressive, use lots of gestures, eye rolling and sometimes they draw on the ground. Some

of the listeners mouth the words to the stories, their eyes fixed on the speaker. There are master storytellers, so popular you can't see them for the crowd and then there are postulant storytellers who have no one but continue their litany in the hope that one day they too will build up a following.

The best place to observe the square is from upstairs at the famous Argana Café. Although it looks like a confusing festival of smoke, food stalls and shouting people, there is actually an order to Djemaa el Fna. Sheep's head stalls are together, harira soup stalls are together, fish stalls, tagine and salad, kebabs, freshly squeezed orange juice. Rachida is the only woman who has a stall of all the dozens and dozens there that are manned by men. She is big, smiling and generous, piling my plate up with her steaming tagine as I perch on a long wooden seat, squashed in with everyone else. Quarters of lemon and little bowls of harissa are thrown in front of you along with a few sheets of kitchen paper and you dig in, preferably with your fingers. They set up their stalls at 5 p.m. which leads one to suppose that by 9 p.m. food would have been sitting there all evening in the heat. I could feel my guts fulminating just looking at it but I wasn't worried as there must have been a huge turnover. All the salads were arranged in beautiful designs along with grilled eggplants, bread, couscous, fizzy drinks, chopped beetroot, bunches of fresh coriander and bowls of harissa soup. The cooks dress in white with white chef's hats and business is brisk as they loudly insist to all the gazelles that their food far surpasses anyone else's.

Most stalls in the square do kebabs and keftas (meatballs), which are a great old Berber tradition. The mechoui, which you will read about in Chapter Two, is the greatest and most dramatic of all the skewered foods – a whole lamb roasted in a pit or on a spit. As no part of an animal is ever wasted in Morocco, the people are very partial to skewered and roasted offal – liver, kidneys, heart, brains. The intestines and lungs usually go into tagines. When skewering food or making keftas, like making French terrines, it is very important to add lots of fat and salt for flavour and goodness. If there is little fat on the meat they add lumps of mutton or beef fat. Berbers often substitute the fat with caul, which they wrap around the kebab before grilling. Kebabs (which can be made from any meat you like) are usually just skewered and grilled au naturel then sprinkled with salt, pepper and cumin; or they might be swished around in paprika, cumin, chopped onions and parsley and then grilled. You could also use the marinade for mechoui in Chapter Two for kebabs. They are always put into a pocket of bread to eat, sometimes with lemon-thinned harissa dribbled on top. When I was in Fès, a woman told me about her favourite dish which she called 'kebabs-that-are-not-kebabs' and I found it in Marrakech. In this famous Marrakech recipe, Tagine Kebab Meghdor, the meat is marinated and grilled on skewers then cooked in a tagine with lots of butter and eggs – too divine.

Tagine Kebab Meghdor

Serves 6

1 kg boned shoulder of lamb, cut into 2.5-cm pieces
   (don't cut off any fat)

For the chermoula:
250 g onion (roughly), grated
sea salt and freshly ground black pepper
3 cloves garlic, smashed
2 tbsp olive oil

For the tagine:
50 ml (¼ cup) butter
handful parsley, chopped
handful fresh coriander, chopped
1 tsp ground cumin
1 tsp sweet paprika
¼ tsp chilli powder
1 cinnamon stick
juice of 1 lemon
6 eggs

1. Marinate the lamb with half the grated onion and the salt, pepper, garlic and oil. Leave for half an hour.
2. Thread lamb on six skewers or leave loose. Grill or fry on high heat until seared on both sides.
3. Heat the butter in the base of a tagine dish. Add the lamb, remaining onion, herbs and spices. Barely cover with water and simmer, partially covered by the tagine lid for three-quarters of an hour. This can be done in the oven or on the stove top. There should be quite a bit of sauce.
4. Sprinkle the tagine with lemon juice and carefully break the eggs in. Cover and poach eggs until cooked. Place directly on the table from the oven and eat with lots of Moroccan bread.

Kefta

In Morocco they grind the kefta meat very finely so get your butcher to do it on the smallest grind.

Serves 6 as finger food

600 g ground beef or lamb
100 g ground beef or lamb fat
1 tsp ground cumin
1 tsp Ras el-Hanout (see page 110)
2 tsp salt
¼ cup mint, freshly chopped
1 small onion, grated

1. Knead all ingredients together very well, then let sit for half an hour to take on the flavourings.
2. Wet your hands and shape keftas into little footballs. Slide onto skewers. If you're not using skewers, they can just be fried as is.
3. Grill quickly on both sides until cooked to your liking. Moroccans like them well done; I like them medium-rare.

One day a beautiful Algerian man wandered into the kitchen of my restaurant in Paris and taught me his mother's favourite kefta recipe. There is a Moroccan version called Kefta Ma'ammra.

Kefta and Stuffed Courgettes

Serves 6

For the sauce:
300 g dried chickpeas
pinch bicarbonate of soda
2 medium onions, finely sliced
2 tbsp extra virgin olive oil
2 tsp Ras el-Hanout (see page 110)
2 good pinches of saffron, soaked in
 a little hot water for 10 minutes

1 tsp honey
1 tsp ground cumin
1 tsp salt
1 tsp harissa
2 x 400-g tins of peeled Italian tomatoes

1. Cover chickpeas with water. Add bicarbonate of soda and soak overnight.
2. In a large, heavy-based pot, fry onions in olive oil until golden and melting.
3. Add remaining ingredients and stir in, then add chickpeas and simmer for an hour or until chickpeas are cooked.

For the kefta and courgettes:
1 kg finely ground lamb
½ cup parsley, finely chopped
1 tsp Ras el-Hanout (see page 110)
2 tsp salt
1 egg, beaten
½ onion, finely chopped
600 g small courgettes

1. Mix lamb, parsley, ras el-hanout, salt, egg and onion together with your hands.
2. Wash courgettes and cut into 5-cm pieces. Hollow out with an apple corer and stuff with lamb mixture.
3. Roll remaining mixture into little balls.
4. Drop these and the stuffed courgettes into the sauce and cook gently for 15 minutes.

Serve with wedges of lemon to squeeze over.

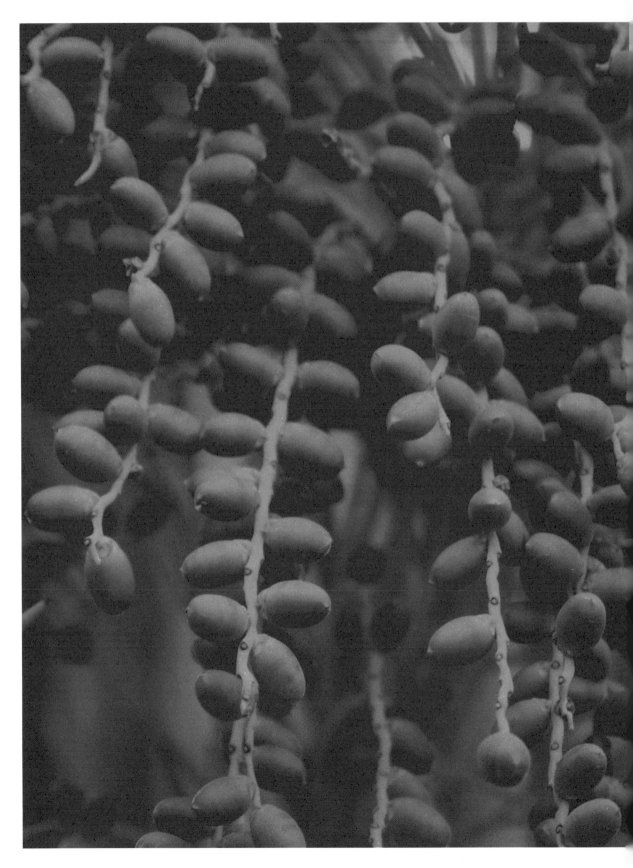

During the day, Djemaa el Fna Square is much quieter and full of dried fruit and orange juice stands. Eight varieties of plump, juicy dates and every kind of dried fruit imaginable – figs, apricots, raisins, prunes – call out to you. Dates occupy a very important place in the agricultural and festive calender of the Berbers and most villages still use ancestral methods to prepare dates for sale. The récolte runs from August through October, is terrifyingly hard work and lasts from sunrise until sunset. This is the time of year they make the money that has to last the rest of the year. Like olive and fig trees and grape vines, date palms last a very long time, sometimes growing to heights of thirty metres. The growers climb up the trees barefoot and with a sort of machete slice bunches of dates off, or if they're very ripe they just bang them off. The dates fall onto a canvas sheet at the shady foot of the tree. The fruit is very mielleux, a lovely word meaning very sugary and ripe. The canvas is pulled so that the dates go to the side, thus not to be damaged by the next fall.

The methods for drying dates depend on the variety. The boussekri with firm, very sweet flesh is removed from the stalk and dried naturally in the air. Crushed for a snack, it is called l'hriss and Moroccans love it with mint tea, yoghurt or water. The majhoul, which are less sweet, are dried on rooftops in the late afternoon sun, still on their stalks. The boufggous, the softest, most honeyed dates, are the most fragile and susceptible to worms and rotting. They are plunged into cumin-flavoured water then sealed in hermetic bags. For personal use in the villages, the fruit is put in big earthenware jars, which are well sealed and then buried because, like olive oil, air and light are the big enemies to dates. Called 'the buried ones', these dates have a strong smell and bitter taste from the alcohol which forms during the fermentation of the fruit's sugar. Dates are used to feed cows, goats and sheep and the stones are pulverised into a powder resembling coffee. This is drunk with water to aid digestion. Unfortunately, the palm groves are shrinking, in part because of immigration – many people don't see a future in working the soil. In 1947 there were 85,000 hectares in production; now there are only 44,000, due mainly to an incurable disease and prolonged drought. Nevertheless, the date groves are the key to the desert ecosystem of the sub-Sahara and assure a microclimate for fresh market gardening. They are also key in the salads, lamb tagines and seven-vegetable couscous I like eating. Which brings me to the souk . . .

Bordering the square is an immense maze of markets or quissrya (covered souks), which wink and beckon like Aladdin's cave. As I wandered through, there was always Arabic music wafting out of corners and shops and balconies. Every so often I would stop and ask what it was and the answer was either that someone was singing the Koran or it was Oum Kalsoum singing. Arab music is very difficult for the Western ear to understand; it is not made up of the same melodic systems we are accustomed to. Listening to this music for the first time was strange for me because it was so different – almost like religious chanting. The instruments sounded unfamiliar and 'swooney' is the only way I can describe it. It is very florid singing with much improvisation – very beautiful.

I had first met Dar Tasmayoun's owner Florence Verley when I was in Marrakech writing *Sirocco*. I looked her up again while doing the recce for this culinary adventure and discovered she had moved out of the medina and built the fabulous Dar Tasmayoun out in the bucolic bled at the foothills of the Atlas Mountains. David and I looked at several country places for our clients and listlessly turned them all down – we didn't even know why, we just knew they weren't hitting the YES button. This was not helped by the fact we were being driven around in an old Mercedes with no air-conditioning and enough leaking gas to poison a camel. I won't even mention the suspension which resulted in the complete rearrangement of our pelvic bones. Finally we called Florence, saw Dar Tasmayoun and knew immediately that it was the one, even though it had only been open a year. We drove up and down the dusty road, practically semi-conscious from the fumes, looking for a sign Florence had said she would put out (but had forgotten to) and finally found it. We drove up the long drive past her organic garden and menagerie of birds, bunnies, ducks and baa lambs to a gorgeous, ochre-coloured, rammed earth mansion.

Florence is a handsome Parisian with perceptive blue eyes and short silver hair who, like David, has a penchant for linen. Her reserved, careful manner made me a bit scared of her but David laid on the charm and I left him to it. In retrospect I think that Florence couldn't understand me at all – French people are either enchanted by or disparaging of New Zealanders' openness and friendliness. In Paris, it would take you a long time to make French friends but when French people emigrate to New Zealand the first thing they notice is how easy it is to do business and how quickly they get invited to dinner at people's homes. Florence is an haute bourgeois intellectual with a very good accent and I am a middle-class artist with a loud voice. David is a man from a posh background: he was the perfect go-between.

I really had no idea to what point Florence didn't understand our cultural differences until the gastronomads turned up with their luggage, jokes and easy temperaments. I had two groups on separate visits and Florence, with a drink in one hand and cigarette in the other, spent hours asking us questions about our lives, attitudes and manner of relating to the world. She was fascinated that a group of complete strangers could integrate, get along and talk about intimate things with each other so quickly. It seemed to her that we must have met before – how could human beings be so naïve, so ready to let go at the drop of a hat, so guileless? You don't grab French people and hug them for God's sake. Our gastronomads greeted everyone by kissing them and touching their arms, something you would only do if you know someone well. The ones who could speak a skerrick of French immediately dropped the vous and went straight to tu. When I told Florence New Zealanders see themselves as rather introverted and emotionally buttoned-up and envy the French their emotionality, she burst out laughing. Florence is good at picking up speech and languages; she communicates with Radiga the cook in Arabic and was soon having conversations in English with the gastronomads.

Upon arrival at the house, everyone gasped as they wandered around the four inner courtyards – full of flowers, pomegranates and birds – in and out of the large bedrooms, up and down the stairs to the two towers to see the magnificent view and then into the kitchen to meet Florence, Radiga the shy cook and Mohamed the homme à tout faire (gardener, chief rabbit throat slitter, singer, bird strangler, storyteller and person-not-possesed-of-one-shy-bone-in-his-body). Radiga is a tall, quiet Berber woman with long brown fingers, a beautiful face and surprisingly sophisticated cooking skills. These had come not only from her mother but also from her years of working in the United Arab Emirates, where she learned how to cook Middle Eastern dishes. On our first visit she made a perfect taboulé with lots of mint and parsley and little cracked wheat, the way it should be. She normally dresses in a dowdy smock and apron and always has her long hair covered with a scarf, but when she realised she was being filmed, she changed into a flamboyant, flowery Middle Eastern robe. Having scanned the kitchen, the gastronomads then jumped into their swimsuits and plunged into the pool to cool down. Jane wandered around, memorising every single thing of interest and Jeff got his camera set up for the sunset, which comes early in summer. I hung around the kitchen as usual, drinking mint tea and watching Radiga. If you say to New Zealanders and Australians, 'Would you like a cup of tea or a glass of water?', they look at you as if you have forgotten to take your medication – David had to quickly set to arranging the bar. He set up at the open pool house and spent the next three days making inordinate quantities of gin and tonic. He was lucky to get out of there long enough to eat. With our first group we had so many people that David had to sleep outside in the pool shed, a sacrifice he reminds me of every time he has a gin.

Dar Tasmayoun is natural, rustic and luxurious and the interiors make constant reference to the beauty of Moroccan culture. Florence has an impeccable sense for what's just right and she's sourced lovely old decorative pieces from Marrakech and the surrounding countryside, along with lots of interesting odds and ends from which she creates remarkably original sculptural pieces. The story of this house is an inspiring one. Florence was a speech therapist in her native Paris and she'd been to Morocco on vacation. Quite naturally, she says, it got under her skin. She visited Morocco several times and was seduced by the architecture, handcrafts and the Moroccan people's appreciation of nature. One morning she woke up in her home in Paris and thought, This is it, I'm moving to Marrakech. She lived in the medina for three years but it became too closed in and she needed space. This is why she moved to the country – where it is open, pure, authentic and surrounded by farms. For me, the most magical thing about Florence's life is that she grows wheat to make her own flour in a little field right outside her front door.

Florence designed and built the house herself with the help of local workers. She'd never done anything like this before and neither had they – it was made by hand with almost no tools. She became quite the sensation locally! All they used were hammers, nails, buckets made from old tires and plumber's wire to hold together the primitive work platform, which was made from half-rotten old planks. People found her very unusual because she was a single woman doing this on her own and because she was building a mud house, which they considered backward. Moroccans love modern stuff – they build all new houses out of concrete. She wanted to do it the traditional way because (a) she loved the architecture of ancient rammed earth dwellings; and (b) it is more environmentally friendly. All through this area are imposing casbahs (citadels) made entirely from earth and straw. You make the mud bricks in a wooden mould then leave them to dry in the sun. Although it was hard work, Florence is very pleased with how the house turned out and wants it to reflect her personality, as well as assimilate the energy of passing guests. She thinks it's good to break from routine, to change your life and do something completely different – it is creative and rewarding. When I ask her about the future, she says she lives in the present and what happens, happens. She considers herself very lucky in finding Radiga and Mohamed – they are enthusiastic, gentle and trustworthy.

Our welcome dinner of garden salads, harira soup, lamb tagine with prunes and fruit from the garden was served out at the pool house to the accompaniment of local Berber musicians. David had placed little candles all the way around the large swimming pool because you never know with gin and tonic – starry, starry night can quickly become scary, scary night. Berber music is very ancient village folk music and consists of poems and chants. It can also be fused with rock. The Rolling Stones, Led Zeppelin and William Burroughs have all experimented with Berber musicians. Cameraman Jeff, also a musician, fixed up their crappy amp and they set to with guitar, mandolin and percussion, passing the mandolin over to Jeff for his rendition of Madonna's 'Ray of Light'. Berber music is predominantly percussion but can also have a kanza, a long rectangular base guitar type instrument; quarbas or hand cymbals; and the imzhad, a string instrument like a violin. It is very fast, loud and rhythmic. Moroccans, both men and women, cannot hear one beat of this music without jumping up to sing and dance. The dancing is a very fast stamping from foot to foot – almost like a toddler throwing a tantrum – with the arms held up and hands clapping. There's no such thing as getting tired – you do it all night. Mohamed was in his element – every time this music started up, so did he.

The chief ingredients in harira soup vary but seem to be tomatoes, lentils, herbs, spices and lamb broth; it can also have chickpeas, rice and noodles. It is thickened with flour and lemon juice is squeezed over it just before eating. Harira soup is often accompanied by shabbakiya, a soft, honeyed cake. Moroccans often serve sweet pastries at the beginning of a meal, which is most unusual to the European palate. To be asked to eat a sweet pastry with a savoury soup takes your taste buds to the limit of what they can endure. We don't really expect to start a meal with sugar as sugar closes off the appetite, rather than opening it up. For the same reason it is ill-advised to serve cheese as finger food before a meal – protein fills you up so you are disinclined to participate in the main act. Harira is traditionally eaten at the end of the day to break the fast during Ramadan but is also eaten all year round, especially in the evening. Moroccans consume it with dates, milk and coffee. Some people use yeast instead of flour to thicken the soup, or mix flour with water and leave it to stand and ferment for a day. This gives a slightly bitter, musky taste.

Harira

Serves 6

1 tbsp smen (rancid butter) or 2 tbsp butter or olive oil
2 onions (250 g), chopped
2 tbsp celery leaves, chopped
½ cup parsley, chopped
1 tsp turmeric
1 tsp salt
freshly ground white pepper
½ tsp cinnamon
2 pinches saffron
½ tsp paprika
500 g lamb in 1-cm cubes
giblets and trimmings of 1 chicken
½ cup green lentils
2 tbsp fresh coriander, chopped
1 kg very ripe tomatoes, peeled, deseeded and puréed
    or 2 x 400-g tins of tomatoes
2 tbsp tomato paste
1 litre lamb or chicken stock or water
3 tbsp flour
lemon wedges

1. Heat fat in a large pot and sauté the onions, celery leaves, parsley
   and turmeric for about five minutes. Then add salt, pepper, cinnamon,
   saffron, paprika, lamb and chicken bits. Continue sautéing until
   golden, for about fifteen minutes.
2. Add lentils, coriander, tomatoes, tomato paste and stock or water.
   Bring to boil then lower heat to a simmer. Cover and cook for half
   an hour or until lentils are soft.
3. Whisk flour with enough water to make a runny paste and add, stirring
   all the time, to the soup. Cook for about five minutes.

Serve in bowls with lemon wedges on the side.

After a breakfast of m'lawi (home-made Moroccan pancakes), Radiga's bread, jam, fruit, mint tea and coffee, we handed out recipe sheets and the flash aprons David had designed and fell into line in the large kitchen to be taught how to make one of the most famous and rich dishes in the whole Moroccan repertoire: pigeon pastilla.

I first tasted pigeon pastilla at the home of a gorgeous woman called Nadia in the coastal town of Larache, which is called the blue town after all the blue doors and shutters. Nadia had just gotten a girl in to henna my feet and I was sitting there with my pegs stuck out like a chicken as I waited for them to dry. They had already fed me Moroccan salads and a huge perfectly crunchy-on-the-bottom paella, so when the pastilla turned up I almost fainted with anxiety that I wouldn't do it justice. As at all meals, far too much food was served, which for Moroccans means just enough. There must be abundance, an embarrassment of riches; they must be able to say with pride, 'But you've eaten nothing.' In Western culture, we make more or less enough because our mothers said, 'Waste not, want not.' In Moroccan culture, giving and generosity is everything and nothing is wasted, because out the back there are armies of servants and children who will eat it all up.

To get a home-made pastilla is really something. In fact anything home-made in Morocco is usually ten times better than what you get at a restaurant. In came a very large, round, flat pie. It was full of ground almonds, pigeon (or chicken), loads of eggs mixed with lemon juice, spices, layers of warka and dusted with cinnamon and icing sugar. Pastilla is typical of the lyricism of Moroccan cuisine. It had humble origins as a simple Berber dish of chicken cooked with saffron and butter. When the Arabs brought the art of pastry making from Persia, it was combined with their pastry called trid. Then the Jews from Andalusia came along and embellished it even more until it ended up being the extravagant complex pastilla served to me. This mixing of sweet and savoury is very typical of the Andalusian heritage. Nadia's cook had no recipes for her dishes; she measured nothing, weighed nothing – she had an extraordinary memory and a good eye and nose. Moroccan women don't write anything down as their culinary skills are inherited from their mothers and aunts.

There are two other pastillas: seafood pastilla and keneffa or sweet milk pastilla. In the seafood one I ate at the famous Palais Fès restaurant in Fès, the layers of warka pastry are filled with fish, shrimp, parsley, coriander, a little chilli and vermicelli and it is served with lemon wedges. Purists consider, slightly sneeringly, seafood pastilla to be a modern and untraditional dish; I think it's absolutely delicious and not nearly as rich and exhausting as a pigeon pastilla.

Seafood Pastilla

For this recipe, you'll need a 30-cm low-sided baking dish, like a pizza or paella pan.

Serves 12 as a starter. Recipe can be halved.

100 g rice vermicelli
500 g shrimps or prawns, shelled and deveined
500 g firm white fish
2 tbsp butter or olive oil
1 small onion, finely chopped
2 cloves garlic, chopped
¼ tsp chilli powder
½ tsp paprika
1 tsp salt
freshly ground black pepper
2 bay leaves
2 tbsp parsley, chopped
2 tbsp coriander, chopped
12 sheets warka or filo pastry
melted butter or oil in a spray can
lots of lemon wedges

1. Soak vermicelli in boiling water for five minutes until soft. With scissors, cut into little pieces.
2. Chop shrimps or prawns into small pieces and cube fish. Heat butter or oil in a pan and sauté onion and garlic for about five minutes. Add the chilli, paprika, salt, pepper and bay leaves. Continue cooking for five minutes.
3. Add shrimps or prawns and fish to the pan, along with parsley and coriander. Stir in and cook gently until just done – maybe five minutes.
4. Add vermicelli, remove from the heat and allow to cool.

5. Preheat the oven to 180 °C (355 °F).
6. Keep pastry sheets covered in a slightly damp cloth while you are working. Grease baking dish and line with six pastry sheets, brushing each one generously with butter. Arrange them so they overlap the sides and hang over.
7. Pour in seafood filling. Fold the overlapping sheets over. Now butter the remaining sheets. Place them on top, overlapping, then tuck them in under the pie. Brush the top with butter or spray with oil.
8. Bake in the oven for about half an hour or until golden.

*Moroccans dive into the centre of the pie with their fingers.
Otherwise it can be cut into slices and served with lemon wedges.*

Milk pastilla is completely different again. It is also modern and comes in many different arrangements. I make it in separate, open layers, which is the way I first ate it at Dar Mima restaurant in Marrakech. A little like the French mille-feuilles, the flamboyant milk pastilla is designed to disintegrate when you plunge a fork into it, mess up your lipstick and decorate the table with dozens of shards of golden pastry. It is constructed of layers of deep-fried warka sheets in triangles with almond pastry cream tinted with orange blossom water and grilled chopped almonds. This is built up high, layer upon layer – just like Moroccan life. I was ethically disinclined to violently reduce to mush what the cook had so painstakingly built up into art. After studying the matter closely, I devised a manner of eating it perfectly: I lifted off a triangle of pastry covered in cream and nuts and ate it with my hands, then moved on to the next layer. Thus saving my and the cook's reputation. In this cooking was the unmistakable touch of French hands – someone restrained was guiding the kitchen. The hospitality at Dar Mima was not the usual over-the-top Moroccan style, but quieter and more sophisticated.

Milk Pastilla

You can make everything in advance but don't put it together until the last minute or the pastilla will go soggy.

Serves 4

For the milk sauce or keneffa:
3 cups milk
3 tbsp cornflour
4 tbsp icing sugar
pinch of salt
½ a vanilla pod slit open or ¼ tsp real vanilla extract
1 tbsp rose or orange flower water

1. Take half a cup of the milk, add the cornflour and stir to a paste.
2. Put the remaining milk, icing sugar, salt and vanilla into a pot and bring to a simmer. Pour the cornflour mixture in, stirring constantly with a wooden spoon and simmer until thick – about 3 minutes.
3. Remove from the heat and stir in the flower water. Transfer to a bowl and rub butter over the surface to prevent a skin forming.

For the almonds:
100 g blanched almonds
1 tbsp butter
2 tbsp icing sugar
½ tsp cinnamon

1. Fry the almonds in the butter until golden – about 5 minutes. Chop coarsely and toss in a bowl with the icing sugar and cinnamon.

For the pastry:
½ cup vegetable oil
6 sheets warka or spring roll pastry
kitchen paper

1. Heat the oil in a large frying-pan and quickly fry the pastry sheets one by one until they go crispy. Place on kitchen paper.

To put the pastilla together:

1. Place a pastry sheet on a serving dish, spread with some milk sauce and sprinkle with almond mixture. Repeat this until everything is used up.
2. Dust with icing sugar and serve immediately. Cut in four with a sharp knife – it will break a bit but is utterly light and delicious.

Back to the pigeon pastilla. I bought the two principal ingredients – pigeons and warka pastry – at the mellah (Jewish quarter) market. The mellah is more expensive than other markets but the quality of the produce is very high. It is full of fascinating shops stuffed full of pyramids of spices, such as red paprika, ras el-hanout, a special mixture containing anything from five to twenty-five spices, pale green aniseed, fenugreek, brick-coloured cayenne, black pepper, pale mustard-coloured ginger, bright yellow turmeric, olive green cumin and chocolate-coloured cinnamon. It's very hard not to just plunge your hands into the pyramids when you see such huge amounts of colour and are so entranced by the perfumes. Small boxes of saffron are there along with armfuls of fresh parsley, mint and coriander. Piles of almonds, citrus, preserved lemons; hillocks of shining black olives marinating in lemons, cayenne and parsley; green olives tossed with secret mountain herbs; big bowls of harissa. The vegetable shops have kumquats, limes, grapes, red onions, nutty red Moroccan potatoes, melons, pomegranates and baby pineapples. The mellah has the best butcher shops in the medina and the butchers are cordial and helpful. In the market you witness the life (and death) cycle of chickens, rabbits, guinea hens and pigeons in the space of a few stalls. In one shop, you can buy eggs from a big basket on the floor, then move to the pigeon cages to chose your birds. While the stallholder passes the time of day with you, the birds are taken to the head chopping room in another stall a few metres away. The bird's cavity is then emptied, ignoble bits chucked on the floor, feathers plucked and the warm, empty body handed back to you wrapped in paper. You should only choose very young pigeons of three months old. An older pigeon you might use for a different dish but for a pastilla it has to be very tender. For a big pastilla like the one I'm going to make I'll probably need half a dozen pigeons. Something worth noting if you are making a pastilla at home is that farmed pigeons available in Western countries are always big but are still perfectly tender.

With my warm pigeons in my basket, I next visit the warka stand to buy those heavenly, translucent, parchment pastry sheets. You could make this fragile steamed pastry at home, but I have to say that like me most Moroccan cooks are more than happy to purchase their warka from specialist makers. In a corner of the mellah market, two young men spend all day patiently making hundreds of round warka leaves. First you make the dough, which is just flour, water, salt and a tiny bit of vinegar. You need to use a very hard flour, high in gluten. It is a wet, elastic dough which you work for about five minutes in a beating motion with the fingers, then rest in the fridge for forty-five minutes. Warka is cooked by steaming so you get a big pot of simmering water and place an inverted tobsil (large round pan with a shallow lip) or other inverted shallow pan on top. Break off a piece of pastry and dab it quickly and delicately onto the heated pan in a rhythmic, circular pattern. The pastry dries out immediately, a bit like egg white, and is peeled off straight away, placed on top of the pile and brushed with oil. And that's it. Interestingly, this is exactly the way I observed the Vietnamese and Chinese making rice paper so you can see where this technique came from – probably Marco Polo on the Silk Road. There is a revolutionary cheat method of making warka: you make the pastry even wetter and paint it on the heated pan with a large pastry brush. This method works brilliantly and is much less terrifying.

The kitchen at Dar Tasmayoun is large and airy with green tiles and a round table in the centre. Radiga and I were going to be working together to teach the recipes. Or so I thought. Radiga has the nature of Mother Theresa – serene, patient and loving – but with a core of steel. Every day she turned up with her beautiful smile, colourful dress and scarf wrapped around her head. Every day I thought I was going to be teaching something and every day it was Radiga who taught something. There are approximately three people in the world who have crossed me and they all died a horrible death. Radiga, very gently and softly, made it clear (she doesn't speak French or English) that there was no way in a million years I could know what I was talking about in terms of the food she has been making all her life. I became very sensitive to her body language and could recognise tiny facial movements, shifts in the position of her shoulders and a tensing of her beautiful brown hands, which indicated that she didn't agree with my method. Florence, who is not that interested in cooking, leaned on the doorway of the kitchen, smoking and watching the performance between Radiga and me with amusement. The students, who were all revved up in their new aprons, sipped water and watched, fascinated. David hid behind the gin and tonic counter and Jeff and Jane just kept rolling that camera.

A scene that illustrates my relationship with Radiga took place during the making of the pastilla, over which we nearly came to blows (well, not really). You see, I have been making pastilla for years, have tasted it many times and thought I was pretty good at making it. At one point in a pastilla you have to cook the eggs and lemon juice together and I usually do it to a light scrambled stage – Radiga went much further and completely dried it out. She didn't want to use the cinnamon I had bought; she wanted to use her own . . . the soft battle of the wills continued like a cotton wool tug-of-war.

The gastronomads Joan, Jeanne, Rona, Errol and Jan had never emptied pigeons before but they rolled up their sleeves and pulled out the guts and lungs, carefully keeping the delicious livers, kidneys and hearts for the stew. I was determined that everyone would understand Moroccan food from the very beginning of the food chain to the moment they put it in their mouths. None of them is a heavy-duty cook – they're more like home cooks who love adventures – but they try anything and constantly voice their appreciation of the knowledge Radiga and I are imparting to them. Most cooking schools in Marrakech have absolutely hopeless recipe sheets but because I write recipes for a living, ours are always very clear and orderly. Nevertheless, if anyone says, 'It says here, Peta, that it's half a teaspoon of cinnamon, not a teaspoon', I just tell them to shut up.

Finally, the pastilla was made and we packed it and delicious sandwiches Radiga had prepared into baskets to take on a picnic. Mohamed insisted on carrying almost everything himself and we set off in the cars with rosé, tea, fruit, dates, colourful rugs and cheerful dispositions. We found a wide and verdant valley with a little lake and lay the giant Moroccan tent base down. Mohamed sat quietly by, declaring that he had had his one meal a day, thank you, as we ate with our fingers, listened to the birds, lay under the trees on the red earth and scanned the splendid and painterly landscape of the Atlas Mountains. David had already gone native and was wearing a purple scarf wrapped around his head like Mohammed. The gastronomads took to eating with their hands and drinking rosé in the middle of nowhere like ducks to water.

Moroccans don't really do picnics and are slightly mystified by the Western need to pack everything up, go outside and eat it, then come back inside again. The closest they get is to visit the roof of their house at night, where they practically live during the summer – cooking, eating, sipping tea, watching television and sleeping. Why would you drag it all off under some tree in the middle of nowhere?

Pigeon Pastilla

This pie is often made with chicken. Although a savoury dish, it is very sweet in Morocco. I have cut out the sugar, but if you prefer it, you can add half a cup to the ground almonds. It is served as a starter and Moroccans eat it with their fingers. You can find spring roll pastry in the frozen section of the supermarket, which is the closest thing to warka. You can also use filo pastry. This recipe is for individual pastillas but you can make one big one, too.

Makes 10 individual pastillas

3 pigeons or 1 small chicken weighing 1–1.5 kg
1 medium onion, finely chopped
4 cloves garlic, finely chopped
2 pinches saffron, soaked in a little hot water for half an hour
¼ tsp turmeric
1 tsp dried ginger
2 cinnamon sticks
1 tsp ground cumin
1 tsp freshly ground black pepper
½ tsp salt
1 tbsp olive oil
1 cup water
140 g (¾ cup) whole blanched almonds
¼ cup lemon juice
6 eggs, beaten
¼ cup coriander, chopped
¼ cup parsley, chopped
8 sheets warka or 1 packet spring roll pastry
   (20 x 20 cm, containing 20 sheets) or filo

For the garnish:
icing sugar
ground cinnamon

1. Quarter chicken or leave pigeons whole and place in a pot with the onion, garlic, saffron, turmeric, ginger, cinnamon, cumin, pepper, salt, oil and water. Bring to the boil, cover and simmer for an hour.

2. Heat a little extra oil in a pan and brown almonds lightly. When cool, grind to a powder in a food processor. Add some sugar now if you wish.

3. Remove poultry and cinnamon sticks from cooking liquid and put aside to cool. Boil to reduce sauce by half. Lower heat, add lemon juice and beaten eggs and stir until just scrambled. Add coriander and parsley and cool over a colander so any excess fluid can run out.

4. Pull all flesh off poultry bones and shred coarsely. Up to this stage the pastilla can be prepared in advance.

5. Lay out 10 pastry sheets on a work surface and have the other 10 ready. Brush or spray olive oil on them. Divide poultry into 10 portions and place in a mound at the centre of each pastry sheet. On top of poultry, spoon egg mixture, then 2 tbsp of ground almonds for each pastilla.

6. Fold overlapping pastry sheet around filling to form a round pie. Turn over so that the folds are on the bottom and repeat with another sheet, spraying it with oil.

7. Place pastillas on an oiled baking sheet. Brush with more olive oil and fan bake at 180 °C (355 °F) for 20 minutes until golden.

Dust pastillas with icing sugar and make criss-cross lines of cinnamon over the top. Serve with Moroccan bread.

Previous: *Me and Mohamed*
Above: *Florence building her mud house*
Left and right: *Dar Tasmayoun*

Top left: *David and Mohamed*
Bottom left: *The gastronomads*
Above: *Radiga*
Following: *Mohamed's son Mustapha*

Chapter Two
Méchoui, Couscous & Tangia

Marrakech is very much about meat. There's no point pretending that animal carcasses are not hanging in front of you in the souk. I was most interested to find out why the fresh carcasses everywhere in the souk didn't stink, didn't attract many flies and didn't bleed in spite of no refrigeration. The answer is halal butchering – all carcasses are bled in the Muslim tradition and the meat eaten quickly. Meat is integral to the Moroccan diet. There's no real concept of vegetarianism in the Moroccan psyche – if you can afford to eat meat, why would you choose not to eat it? It's the backbone of Moroccan cuisine, providing protein and flavour. There are thousands of recipes handed down through generations for every imaginable part of a beast – be it lamb, goat, beef, camel, poultry or game. On my first visit to Marrakech, I hired a guide to show me the secret dens in the medina. My guide was deliciously dark, softly spoken, calm, patient and a chain smoker. He listened carefully to what I was most interested in seeing and never once mentioned that there was more to the medina than eating. Wherever we went, he put his arm out in front of me to protect me from hurtling carts, bikes and donkeys.

The most fabulous discovery for me that day was observing the ritual of a classic Marrakech speciality – tanzhiyya or bachelor's tangia. A tangia is made in a deep clay pot with a wide belly and fairly narrow opening at the top. On each side are two little handles. The bachelor stuffs into it whatever he fancies for lunch: lamb, beef, sometimes camel meat, vegetables and spices like smen (rancid butter), saffron, preserved lemon and cumin. Then he covers the opening with brown paper, attaching it with string. On his way to work in the medina, he stops in at the hammam, and hands it to someone who places the tangia underneath the hammam building in the warm ashes of the oven – the fire that provides all that hot steam for the bath house. It stays there until he picks it up at lunchtime five hours later. Some people put the tangia down the night before. The stew is eaten and the pot never washed – a well-seasoned pot being the secret to a good tangia.

The guide took us down into a dark, hot, black pit called the femachie, which was full of lemon-scented wood shavings. We were under the hammam in an underworld of very kef-stoned men whom we observed at various macabre tasks. One man's duty seemed to be to play the guitar and stoke the fire, while others set themselves to ripping the feet off the shanks of sheep, singeing the hair off in the oven and then cooking them. Others squatted in front of piles of cows' feet and goats' heads, prepping them for cooking. One gentleman was responsible for all the tangia pots of varying sizes, sunken into their purgatory of ashes. In this gentle way, this unspeakably delicious meal is cooked. Every so often the man held a pot up to his ear and shook it to see if the contents were cooked or not. The sound is different as the meat changes consistency. You identify your pot by a little piece of tin imprinted with your number. Later on in the medina, we saw cooked tangias for sale. You asked the vendor what the choice was and made your decision; it is tipped out for you on a plate and served with big chunks of bread. You are directed to the restaurant next door to sit down and eat it with your hands. Everyone washed their hands in a basin at the back before and after the meal. I ate all the bits I could identify and the guide ate the rest, happy that he had been left the best.

Jeff the cameraman/editor is thirty-nine, Canadian, attractive and easy-going. He has been happily married to Jane, the producer/director, for eight years and they have one son. Jane is very slim and pretty, very determined and lots of fun. She is a rock chick in her spare time and Jeff's a musician. For Jeff, less is more and he prefers to just stand and let people do their thing. For Jane, more is less and she can always whittle it down. Jane and Jeff had become friendly with the best slow food operators in the souk – the Boulait family. The brothers Boulait run two stalls: one for the mechoui or pit-roasted lamb; and the other devoted to cooking sheep's heads and tangias. They prep the tangias the night before, then in the morning cross the square to the hammam, laden down with the pots. This happens all over Marrakech every day – stallholders, families and workers all bring their lunch to these convenient communal slow ovens.

Tangia

Serves 4–6

1 kg lamb or hogget leg or shoulder, in very large pieces
1 tbsp butter or smen (rancid butter)
1 tbsp extra virgin olive oil
2 small onions, grated or puréed in a food processor
1½ tbsp garlic, grated with onions
handful of mint or coriander, chopped
handful of parsley, chopped
1 preserved lemon, skin only, sliced
½ tsp ground ginger
½ tsp paprika
½ tsp coriander seeds or powder

1. Preheat oven to 150 °C (300 °F).
2. Mix all ingredients together with your hands and place in an ovenproof dish. Cover and cook for three hours until the meat is absolutely melting. Eat with Moroccan bread.

 A major Moroccan speciality is mechoui or pit-roasted whole lamb. My original guide took me to see one cooking. In the middle of the shop in the souk there is a deep, hot mud pit, into which the whole animal is lowered on a hook. The pit is covered and the beast left in it for at least three hours, being occasionally raised to baste. Now, with this mechoui shop, you had to know exactly when to turn up in order to partake of the heavenly, melting flesh. I was told that the sheep usually came up at 11 a.m. so I made a mental note to turn up the next day. Directly opposite the Café de France on the main square there is an entrance to the medina called Souk Ablouh. You go down where the optician's shop is, and on the right, a little way down, is the mechoui, goat head and tangia land my guide had introduced me to the day before. I arrived just after the lamb had been hauled out of the pit and they were portioning it. Crowds of people gathered around the stall, salivating if I may say so. One man did the cutting, another weighed the meat and put it on a paper-covered tray for you to eat with bread. Another took your money. You pointed out which bits you wanted and paid according to weight. God only knows why I bought so much, but for 80 dirham I got 500 grams' worth of juicy tail, ribs, leg and fat – more than I could possibly consume.

I was directed to the restaurant next door, where I had eaten the tangia, and I climbed up some stairs. There in the cool darkness I ate my feast. It was just like a New Zealand hangi or a Croatian spit-roast or a French gigot de sept heures – unbearably tender, earthy-tasting, and all the better for being consumed with the hands while the juices dribbled down the chin. There is absolutely no doubt that food tastes superior without the cruel interference of stainless steel or silver forks – they keep you from the sensuality of the food and eating. In this restaurant, women came with their families, women friends or husbands. The boy waiter was beside himself to see a foreign woman with red hair eating alone, and every time I spoke to him he just stood and stared at me with his mouth gaping. Downstairs, they wrapped up what I couldn't eat, and I had it cold for dinner with lemon juice, bread and olives.

Jane and Jeff managed to get the Boulait family to agree to be filmed. While the gastronomads and I dreamed of pomegranates and honeyed dates as we lay in our soft beds, Jane and Jeff slung their equipment on and shuffled off to Abdul Boulait's stall at 5 a.m. to shoot the starting of the pit fires. Abdul's father, Omar, is a mechoui veteran of fifty years running a business handed down through the generations. He's known as the best operator in the souk and he's earned it – in his day there was no electricity or water and they had to walk a kilometre to bring water in. While the coals and wood are burning down to the right temperature, Omar watches everything like a hawk. Another brother turns up with the lamb carcasses. Omar does the spine and other chops so the meat roasts evenly. It is sprinkled with salt and cumin and lowered into the oven, which is then sealed with mud. Abdul began helping out at his dad's business as a seven-year-old during the school holidays and even though he received tertiary education in Sweden he counts continuing the family business as his number one priority. He says it's good work and though it's hard he enjoys it very much.

A mechoui can also be spit-roasted and in this method more spices are used. The lamb is brushed inside and out with a paste of butter, salt, pepper, cumin and paprika, a process that is repeated every fifteen minutes throughout the cooking. It can take hours to cook and the 'dry-marinating' is a common method of ensuring a crisp, golden, tasty skin, while the meat inside stays tender and tastes of hogget. There is some evidence to suggest that the Turks introduced skewered meat to Morocco but the Berbers say this is rubbish – that they were cooking whole meat this way long before any Turks wandered in. At a special feast there would usually be kwah served with the mechoui – fresh, cubed lamb liver tossed in cumin, paprika and salt, wrapped in caul or mutton fat and threaded onto skewers and grilled. They commonly place the kebab in a chunk of bread with lashings of chilli sauce – harissa.

Mechoui

It is really worth buying this big cut of lamb as the meat is much more tender roasted in one piece. Invite more people and turn it into a party.

Serves 8–10

1 forequarter lamb (5 kg)
2 tsp ground coriander
2 tsp ground cumin
1 tsp paprika
sea salt
6 tbsp smen (rancid butter) or softened butter

1. Blend all ingredients into a paste.
2. Make deep incisions under foreleg bone along breastplate and rub paste in all over. Let stand for 10 minutes.
3. Preheat oven or barbecue to 250 °C (480 °F). Roast lamb for 15 minutes. Reduce heat to 175 °C (350 °F). Continue cooking for three hours. Baste every 15 minutes with juices from the pan.

Eat with your fingers and have a bowl of ground cumin and sea salt ready for sprinkling.

It was my friend Mimi in Paris who first introduced me to the mysterious, exotic world of henna-tattooed women, mint tea and hot steam, all of which can be found at the hammam. The best hammam or sauna house was at the mosque in the 5th arrondissement. From the Rue Geoffroy-Saint-Hilaire you entered into a sunny garden full of trees, passing through it to the permanent dusk of the exotic Arab tearoom and thence to the inner sanctum. There were alternate days for men and women, thank God, which meant you could completely relax. I found out from Mimi's boyfriend that the men in the hammam wore towels at all times for modesty's sake and to protect themselves from marauding perverts. In unselfconscious contrast, the women flung their clothes off immediately and kept it that way until the last possible minute.

There were three rooms in the Paris mosque hammam: the resting room, the steam room and the sauna room. Having found a mat in the first room on which to lay your possessions, you moved, undressed, into the second large steam room – a womb-like, enchanting space heavy with heat and humidity. Like an ornate chamber from the Arabian Nights, this room had women washing their hair in the marble fountains; North African women, with traditional tattoos on their chins and feet, rubbing henna all over their bodies; and friends massaging each other with hard cloths to remove old skin. Young and old, ugly and breathtakingly beautiful, small and obese were all there, along with Africans, French, Vietnamese, Mimi and moi. Needless to say, the toilets were strictly North African. It's one thing peeing on your feet with shoes on but quite another squatting naked. No toilet paper of course, because you supposedly don't need toilet paper if you are squatting (there is a tap on the toilet wall for that purpose). Coming from a land of anal-compulsive cleanliness on the other side of the world, it took me years to adjust to the Arab toilets found everywhere in France, from chic bars to modern restaurants.

When we had had enough of the ablution in the steam room, we moved on to the third room, the sauna. This small chamber was extremely hot and doing anything more than breathing in it was out of the question. Women just lay around looking bug-eyed, occasionally dousing themselves with freezing water from a hose which lay on the ground. When our hearts recovered sufficiently for us to walk out unaided, we would profit from a professional rub and massage – stumbling over to the massage room to throw ourselves on one of the tables. On the men's days, according to Mimi's boyfriend, having a massage could be a risky business if you were cute. He told me that one day he found a finger probing where it had no business to be.

'Oh my God,' I gasped. 'What did you say?'

'Ouch!'

One third of your body weight is removed by the merciless hands of the masseuse, then you're very ready for the final stage of the ritual: lying catatonic on a mat in the resting room. We rubbed body cream all over ourselves, wrapped ourselves in towels, then lay down and swapped gossip with our neighbours. This room was circular, with typical North African architecture, enchanting glass windows, a marble-tiled floor and Arab rugs. In the middle of the room on a raised dias sat a marble fountain, on the ledge of which rested mint tea in little ornate coloured glasses. You took some when you felt like it, and it was constantly replenished by a harridan crow of a woman whose lack of charm was exceeded only by her lack of good looks. The place smelt of incense, a suggestion of chlorine and steeped mint.

The first hammam I went to in Morocco was in Kenitra with a Moroccan girl, Selma. It was not glamorous like the Paris one – just an ordinary suburban bath house costing 5 dirham to get in, 35 dirham for a massage and scrub, and full of lovely ladies thrilled to see a foreigner with freckled skin and red hair. At the desk, we bought scrubbing gloves, henna, little plastic bags of soft red soap and the services of scrubbers. After our belongings had been stored, the ladies gave us plastic shoes to wear and we went straight into the very hot, steamy room, where we were set upon. Selma had obviously given them instructions to look after me – I wasn't required to lift a finger. No sooner had we sat on the floor than the red soap was rubbed all over us by sumptuous women in nothing but white underpants and white headscarves, which they had wrapped tightly around their heads to keep their long, thick hair out of the way. They filled several buckets with differing temperatures of water and scooped it all over us to wash the soap away. Then they grabbed clumps of henna and rubbed that all over us, including on our faces. This in its turn was brusquely washed off by matter-of-fact hands. The bath ladies were voluptuous mountains of flesh, utterly comfortable in their own bodies and with ours. When these corpulent queens approached our defenceless bodies on the floor, I must admit a look of fear passed over my brow. I'd forgotten how curious it is to be handled all over – and believe me they don't shirk from any crevice! In the process of being turned and every inch of you got at, you fall gently against their bodies – it's like being a child. They take you over.

At this point we were lying on mats on the floor, with the scrubbers sitting on the floor beside us. On went the abrasive gloves (I don't use the word 'abrasive' lightly) and off came our skin in black rolls. 'I think all the skin on my chest has gone. There's a bit left on my thighs,' I groaned to Selma, peering through the thick, humid mist. 'I'll scream if they rub too hard.' Selma was jumping up and down with the stinging of henna mixed with lemon she had rubbed into her skin. We lay there exhausted and zinging – but it wasn't over yet. Another soap washing and rinsing followed, then vigorous hair washing and a deluge poured straight onto our heads. All the time the washers were laughing and joking, grabbing my arms and saying, 'Ça va, Madame, ça va?' They asked Selma lots of questions about me and were most interested to know whether I had had children or not. Later, lying on the mats, I noticed my skin was unbelievably soft and that I felt absolutely rejuvenated. I have since discovered the secret to soft skin is not body cream but regular scrubbing with a hard glove to get the dead skin off.

These days when I go to Marrakech I don't go to the really cheap, grass-roots hammams, basically because they take too long and the average foreigner would need a counsellor afterwards. Medina women, who don't have running water, use them for their weekly wash so they spend half a day there. The city is bursting with all different levels of hammams – my favourites are the mid-range, traditional Hammam Ziani on Riad Zitoune Street, not far from Hôtel du Trésor, and the very luxurious, expensive Les Bains de Marrakech in the Bab Agnaou area. At Ziani you have both Moroccan and foreign customers who are serviced by entirely Moroccan staff. You change into nothing but knickers then move into the steam room, where you wash yourself in a beautiful domed room. From there, you get taken by a masseuse who gives you a good rub, scrub and hair wash, then you move onto the massage room, before getting dressed and having mint tea. There are lots of other women around so modesty is not a required virtue. I like this hammam for its authenticity and attention to detail. For drop-dead excellent pampering either La Maison Arabe or Les Bains de Marrakech are the ticket – think fluffy bathrobes, private rooms, exotic treatments with perfumes and herbs. Like Zen massages with chocolate.

Learning all this, the gastronomads bravely agreed to go to my hammam, stripped off and gave themselves up to the ministrations of the scrubbers. As far as I know they loved it and completely accessed their inner Berber, emerging wet-haired and laughing. They said that even though you get very close to people you spend a week with, you get VERY close in a hammam situation, and that they were glad I made them do such a mad thing.

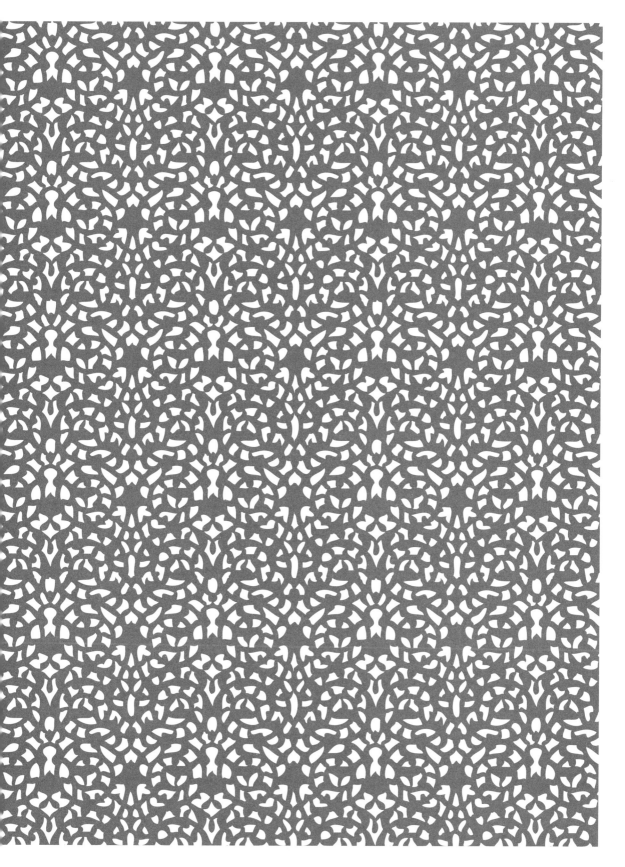

Wherever you wander in Marrakech, you will have access to the famous freshly pressed orange juice. Oranges are grown in huge quantities in Morocco, particularly in the seaside town of Agadir, and everywhere in the markets you see them piled up into precarious orange mountains. They are freshly pressed for breakfast in all hotels and there are several stands for buying fresh juice in the Djemaa el Fna Square. The juice is tart or sweet depending on the time of year – very sweet and very cheap in December. Visitors are fond of the orange juice as they are terrified of drinking the water. If the orange juice in Morocco seems special that's because it is – they put a little orange flower water into it. This is done with most juices – pomegranate, grape, strawberry, watermelon, beetroot, carrot, lemon and lime. The year the temperature got up to 52 °C I drank so much orange juice I almost went into a diabetic coma. I had a wonderful orange and carrot dessert in Essaouira once and here's the recipe.

Orange Soup with Melon

Serves 4

2 cups freshly squeezed orange juice
1 cup freshly made carrot juice
¼ tsp freshly grated nutmeg
2 tbsp cornflour
watermelon or any melon you like, finely cubed
ground nutmeg

1. Heat orange and carrot juices and nutmeg together. Stir in cornflour which has been mixed to a paste with a little water. Continue simmering for 5 minutes.
2. Pour through a sieve then into tea cups or ramekins and allow to cool in the fridge. The soup should be thick but still liquid.

To serve, place cups of soup with teaspoons in them on a large plate. Put a little mound of melon on the plate and make a star next to it with the nutmeg.

The other drink (apart from mint tea) that is synonymous with Morocco is the romantic, heavenly sharbat billooz or almond milk. I first tasted it at Dar Mima restaurant. The owner had personally guided me there down a path lit by little lanterns at footstep level. She welcomed me into a beautifully restored riad with chic, modern Moroccan decor. The colours were cool blue and yellow; sophisticated overhead fans whirred; and the dining areas were secretive and secluded, just as Moroccans love them to be. Upon being seated, I was brought dates soaked in orange water and a little glass of almond milk with rosewater. Then a bowl of rosewater and soap to wash my hands and a snowy white towel to dry them was brought out. I always think of calm and harmony when I drink almond milk.

Sharbat Billooz
Almond Milk

Serves 6

200 g caster sugar
200 g blanched almonds
500 ml water
1 litre whole milk
1 cinnamon stick
50 ml rosewater
ice cubes
ground cinnamon

1. Put half the sugar and almonds into a food processor and blend until very fine.
2. Place in a bowl, cover with the water and stir. Cover bowl with cling film and place in the fridge over night.
3. Put milk, remaining sugar and cinnamon stick in a pot and bring to the boil, stirring. Remove from heat and leave to cool. Skim off any skin that forms, discard cinnamon stick and stir in rosewater.
4. Remove almond mixture from the fridge, give it a stir and strain juice into milk, pressing well to get every last drop. Discard almonds or use them in another recipe.
5. Pour almond milk into a clean bowl or jug, cover with cling film and place in the fridge until cold.

Put a couple of ice cubes in a glass, pour the re-stirred almond milk over and sprinkle with cinnamon.

One of the very important parts of my culinary adventures in Marrakech is eating in a traditional, rural Berber home. No sooner had David and I mentioned this during our recces to Dar Tasmayoun than Mohamed shot his hand up – his wife Latifa would be honoured to cook a meal for us and our clients. Lovely Latifa had married quite a bit older Mohamed at the age of fourteen in an arranged marriage and boy did she luck out. How could anyone have a more perfect husband than the charismatic Mohamed? Devoted to his family, hard-working, funny, multi-talented and intelligent. He can dance, sing, play the fool, farm the land, kill any animal and prepare it for eating and solve any problem. Mohamed's village, like those of countless rural Moroccans, is made of the red ground we walk on. The living conditions are by European standards rudimentary but the welcome is rapturously warm. Latifa and her younger (she has six) children Youssef, Marouane and Kaotar greet us with open arms and kisses and are happy to show us around the compound. Around the back is a donkey for transport, a sheep for future tagines, some chickens and a real Berber sauna.

I saw these ingenious saunas for sale at the souk in Ait Ourir. Here is David's description of it: 'The Berber hammam – in that it is steam, rather than dry heat – is very much a DIY piece of equipment. The frame from the souk is a cylinder approximately 130 centimetres in diameter and 220 centimetres tall, with a slightly domed top. The frame is loosely woven from split bamboo, providing a surface upon which to apply a mixture of earth, and I would imagine lime in order to make it set and not dribble in use. Once your donkey or camel has transported the frame home, it is covered both inside and out with the aforementioned lime plaster mix. There is an entrance in the cylinder approximately 175 centimetres high and 55 centimetres wide. When in use, this is covered by a curtain to prevent steam escaping and the camel or donkey seeing your private parts. The one model I have seen was mounted on a slightly raised platform to allow a small space underneath – occupying no more than 20 per cent of the floor area. Above this, sealed by plaster from the fire – otherwise you would have a rather smoky steam up – is a spot where a pan of modest dimensions, but tending to be wide to maximise evaporation, is filled with water. This is heated to boiling point by the fire underneath and produces steam. A low stool is the only piece of furniture in the hammam and presumably used for sitting on.' How fabulous is that?

Mohamed and Latifa's house comprises various very neat, beautifully painted bedrooms, a salon for entertaining and a courtyard off which there is Latifa's new kitchen. The first time I visited she had a tiny kitchen with just a fire on which to cook all her fabulous meals for six children. Mohamed has now built her a new, much bigger one with a nice floor, shelves, benches and everything. Nevertheless, she still squats on the floor to cook just as she's always done. I asked her if she was thrilled with her new kitchen and with her winsome smile she said, 'Yes, but I was just as happy with the other one.' I would be extremely surprised if Latifa had ever been further than Ait Ourir. She is the sister of Radiga – the sweetness is a family trait. Her and Mohamed have a pretty daughter, Fátima, in her twenties who helped out at the big house during our stay and who has the same serene smile as Radiga. The youngest, very pretty daughter of about eight years old is a chip off Mohamed's block – full of confidence, polite, fun and loves donkey races with her father. The two hospitable eldest sons Mustapha and Khalid helped with serving.

In true Moroccan style, there's no such thing as lunch for half a dozen people, which is why they had also invited their eldest son, Mustapha, who lives in Marrakech, his French partner and their two little children. We all took our shoes off and settled cross-legged into the banquettes around the long low table. At the end of the room, Mohamed was in ecstasy being the host and doing the ceremonial pouring of mint tea. We also got water and Coke, which they love.

Water was passed around for hand-washing. Latifa and Mustapha had prepared a huge salad of crudités, the bread was placed on the table and we dived in. No wine of course – zut alors!

It's quite an invasion as we don't speak Arabic and they don't speak English. They all do the best they can in pigeon French. But it doesn't matter because food is the best way to access a culture – it's the only way as it doesn't need language, it doesn't need an outfit and it doesn't need a book. Food and the knowledge of food is transferred in Morocco through fingertips, hearts and memories. Food is love and when you invite strangers into your home you are saying welcome to my life – I like you.

My gastronomads are very touched that a village family would let them into their home and this meal has been a turning point for them. At the end of the week, in spite of all the outrageous dining experiences they have had, they all said lunch at Mohamed's place was the most humbling and the most interesting – they loved the abundance, the generosity, the simplicity and the freshness of the food. They love that the experience is authentic and that David and I know these people.

If you are not lucky enough to join one of my gastronomic experiences and you find yourself being invited by a Moroccan taxi driver to come to his mother's house for dinner, say yes! You will get the best food presented with integrity and affection. That's what gastronomic travel is about – there's a huge amount of goodwill on both sides. It's not just the people in Morocco being kind, it's that the people who are visiting them also show a lot of kindness and a lot of openness and willingness to have an emotional experience, not just a physical or gastronomic one. That's what the secret is – it goes both ways. Jeff describes Mohamed in this way: 'He's in love with his family; he's in love with life. Imagine putting one of us in his life and saying "Okay, now you're going to make your own honey, look after your family, cook your food on the floor, et cetera." But he's a very happy man in spite of the hard life he's had. That's because he's tied to the land, he's connected to everything, he knows who he is. His wife was arranged for him and somehow they're happy. It's because they are connected to everything else – they are part of a whole picture, whereas we are disconnected in our lives. Although we have easier lives, we are not happier.'

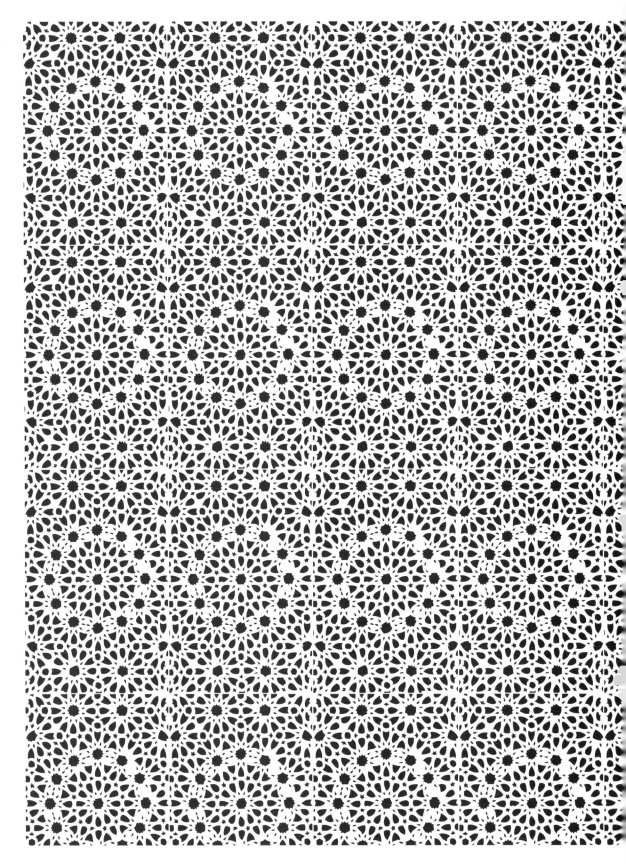

A much-loved and little-talked-about
vegetable very popular in Morocco, which
I have never seen in a restaurant, is the
cardoon or wild artichoke thistle. The head
is very pretty with purple tips, like a regular
artichoke, and it has large stalks. David loves
cardoons, in particular the stalks, which look
a bit like large celery stalks, and he asked for a
tagine with beef and cardoons. When braised
or steamed, they taste divinely like artichokes.
The seeds produce what they call artichoke
oil. Moroccans also use the flower buds and the artichoke head but the
preparation is time-consuming just like a regular artichoke. They say
Fassi women are the best wild thistle cookers because they have the
patience for it.

Friday in Morocco is **couscous** day, family day and big-prayers-at-the-mosque day. When I first arrived in Morocco I was invited to my Kenitra friends Zohra and Mohamed's house for a feast. I was very excited because I had asked to be shown how to make couscous from scratch, which hardly anyone does these days, and the senior aunt in the family, Fátima, who always has lunch with them on Friday, had agreed to give me a lesson. Couscous is a native Berber dish, called by them seksoo or sikuk. A lot of people think couscous is a grain but it's basically baby pasta – traditionally made from white flour, semolina (derived from the purified middle of the wheat grain) and salted water rubbed together. Most Moroccan kitchens, even very modern ones, have a low round table with low stools around it for preparing food. In the old days (and still now sometimes), all the cooking was done on the floor over various burners; in fact everything was done close to the floor – eating, sitting, washing, talking, singing and sleeping.

I loved Fátima. She was a funny, beautiful, very traditional older woman, and in spite of her aches and pains always radiant with smiles and full of caresses and touches. Fátima dyed her fingernails red with henna and wore a lovely white dress with pale green embroidery, an ornate embroidered green belt and her hair tied up in a white scarf. To keep her voluminous sleeves out of the way while cooking, she had on an elastic band, which somehow looped around her neck and through the sleeves.

The low table was pushed out of the way, a sheepskin rug was put on the kitchen floor and Fátima sat down on it. Between her legs Zohra put a huge gas'a (shallow earthenware bowl) and nearby placed a bowl of salted water, a bowl of fine semolina and a bowl of plain flour. This arrangement revealed Fátima's pretty lace bloomers, attached below the knee. 'Oh, I like your bloomers,' I said, smiling. She was very bemused that her dress was of such interest to me and said, 'I hope you don't want a photo of my knickers because I don't wear any.' At this they all shrieked with laughter. She sifted some semolina into the gas'a, then splashed in drops of water, moving it around with her hands, adding a bit of flour, a bit more water, swishing it gently with her fingertips in a rotating motion.

Magically, tiny balls formed. These she tipped into a wide-holed sieve, and then shook them through into a colourful straw platter called a tbaq. This method allows the couscous to expand when steamed without going all gloopy and sticking together. Sounds easy, n'est-ce pas? The truth is, it requires enormous patience, tour de main and of course time. Fátima's finesse, lightness of hand and years and years of knowing exactly the feel of a good rub and consistency of grain is what made this couscous one of such high quality. I got down on the floor after we'd helped her up with much groaning and grunting. Swish as I might, and in spite of every member of the family being chiefs to my one Indian, my result was clumsy next to hers. The family kindly added my grains to the growing pile, which looked enough to feed the King's retinue. Normally, at this stage you would lay it all out in the sun to dry – if you weren't going to eat it immediately.

As Fátima created the tiny balls, Zohra started the first steaming process to cook it. All morning she had been prepping and cooking the meat and vegetable stew to serve with the couscous, and now she placed the couscousiere or steamer over the stew pot and put the first lot of grains in to steam for ten minutes over the fragrant broth. No lid. This she then tipped out onto a platter and combed with her fingers to remove any lumps, gently rubbing in a little olive oil, salt and water. It sat there for ten minutes while she started on the next lot. This process was repeated twice more until all was cooked; the last time, they sometimes rub in smen or butter and rosewater. When the meal was ready to serve, Zohra ladled broth from the stew all over the couscous and placed the meat and vegetables on top. This is the only way to get a really fragrant product, and couscous in Morocco is the best and most refined in North Africa. Prepared this way, it is delicious to eat just on its own. It has strong emotional and religious significance because of its position at the centre of nurturing and sustenance. Here's an interesting connection: couscous has a strong historical similarity to panades, an old Arabic dish made from leftover bread, which is crumbled into stews or soups, and that is just what they do in Andalusia and Portugal with their bread and tomato soups.

I set myself to picking Zohra's brain about her couscous stew. The process is very easy, and they boil the hell out of it – no question of gentle simmering. Mostly the meat is not seared first, and it's just a process of placing all the ingredients in the pot, whacking the heat on and going away. Zohra used big chunks of lamb; the usual combination of Moroccan spices of cumin, paprika, coriander, salt, ginger, imitation saffron (food colouring); and onions, tomatoes and a cup of water. This she cooked for at least an hour. Then the pumpkin, courgettes, carrots, turnips and chickpeas were added at about the time she started steaming the couscous. She never added more than a snippet of chilli to the stew, if at all, because Moroccan cuisine is not hot; it is lyrical, harmonious, complex, pungent. They have a horror of a lack of balance – harmony being the sign of a well-ordered life and healthy mind. All this time Hicham, the son-in-law, was sticking his nose into everything and making comments. In Morocco the male of the species does not usually cook but he is very involved in the sticking-in-of-the-nose, judging, tasting and throwing around of orders and opinions. They say that a man can tell all he needs to know about a woman sight unseen by the way she has cooked a dish. For a society which is still largely covered up and repressed sexually, cooking is a form of communication. For the male middle classes, it is a way of feigning control over the household, when everyone knows it is the woman who captains the ship.

We all sat down to the large platter of couscous placed in the middle of the table in the garden. I noticed, with fear, no utensils. The maid appeared with tablespoons and everyone dug in. Zohra's daughter Latifa said she didn't know how to eat with her hands, but Fátima, who sat herself next to me, did. She gathered couscous, sauce and meat into a neat ball with three fingers of her right hand, then sort of tipped it gently into her mouth with a flip of the thumb – not a crumb anywhere. I tried and tried, decorating the table with the stuff in the process. The hand-rolled, steamed couscous was so light it seemed to levitate above the dish. (When I made it at home my friends said it was like eating perfumed air.) My hosts, chattering non-stop among themselves, were extremely polite and pretended to ignore me dropping grains all over the place.

I enjoyed a very fine couscous in Essaouira once – a couscous royale. I have since copied and taught this couscous many times, so fabulous it is in its layers of flavour and texture. Perfectly steamed couscous provided the thick bed, on top of which were carrots, turnips, succulent chicken and lamb. This was topped with a lava rush of the best caramelised onions I've ever tasted. The sides were decorated with boiled egg halves dipped in sesame seeds and the lot sprinkled with chickpeas and chopped almonds. All this for 62 dirham – at twice the price, it would have been cheap. Slurping down my mint tea, I asked if I could meet the cooks to thank them personally. In the kitchen, the women fled to corners and hid behind their hands; they giggled and giggled when I complimented them. The three handsome waiters stood in a row, smiled proudly and said, 'Berber cuisine, Madame!'

Top left: *Mohamed and Jane*
Bottom left: *Tangias*
Above: *Weighing out the mechoui*
Right: *The mechoui pit*

Top left: *Cooking food in the ashes under the hammam*
Bottom left: *David, Jeff and me*
Above: *Making couscous with the gastronomads*
Top following: *Jeff filming and me*
Bottom following: *Buying kaftans in the medina*

Back at Florence's Dar Tasmayoun, Mohamed takes me on a tour of the expansive, sun-drenched gardens, potager and farmyard. He looks after a hundred olive trees that produce oil every year now; a hundred citrus trees comprising lemons, grapefruit, oranges and clementines; apricot, plum, apple, peach, almond, quince, pomegranate and fig trees; grape vines; decorative trees and bushes including jacaranda, pepper, red bay, roses, white verbena, nightshade, plumbago, cypress, purple ficus, bougainvilleas, palm, hibiscus and cactus. In the potager he looks after lemon grass, absinthe, sage, geranium flowers, rosemary, mint, marjoram and coriander. Winter sees peas, broad beans, onions, carrots, leeks, horseradish, potatoes and turnips; summer sees tomatoes, capsicums, eggplants, green beans, garlic, cauliflower and beetroot. In the little farmyard are rabbits, sometimes a sheep, chickens, guinea hens and ducks. The gastronomads spent lots of time wandering around these gardens and enjoying the tranquillity – I don't think they wanted to leave. In fact, when the time came, they had become so attached to everyone at Dar Tasmayoun that they sang a farewell song and burst into tears (as did I).

I decide that I would like to make a rabbit couscous for our afternoon cooking class so I quickly make my exit in the direction of the kitchen to watch Radiga making couscous. Florence grows wheat so the flour comes from her very own efforts. She sends it to the local miller to be ground and Radiga is very particular about the coarseness she prefers. In other parts of Morocco, couscous can be made from barley or corn, but mostly it is made from flour and semolina. Needless to say, Radiga's couscous was a result of the woman herself – beautifully and carefully made with her sensitive fingers and perfectly judged with her eye and taste buds. She took pleasure in getting us all to have a go at something she considers so elementary. Normally when you are filming a food show, it takes a long time and sequences are done over and over again so you can get close-ups and have everything be perfect. But when you are unplugged and free range and have decided not to get in anyone's way, you just shoot the best you can and enjoy that life has suddenly become more exciting. Mohamed sitting quietly watching. Florence standing, smoking, watching. Fátima assisting in her jeans, apron and head scarf. Gastronomads swishing and rubbing and sifting in amazement. They like participating, not passively watching, and feel they will learn much better if they actually do it themselves. For this class I forgot to put my make-up on. When Jane looked at the rushes she said, 'Make-up on from now on Peta and no you can't get away without it, even if you are under a dark hammam counting sheep's ankles. Thank you. Posture. Make-up. Thank you.'

Couscous

This is how you make couscous from scratch. It is simply a matter of swirling fine semolina, flour, salt and water with the flat of your fingertips until it forms tiny balls, but it is time-consuming and requires years of practice to do properly. Few Moroccans know how to make couscous from scratch. The difference between fresh and dried packet couscous is like the difference between fresh and dry pasta – it tastes plump and tender and airy. To make this recipe, you'll need a large, flat platter with shallow sides – a tea tray is good – and a big, wide-holed sieve like a Chinese bamboo sieve.

Serves 4–6

200 g hard white flour
1 tsp salt
200 g fine semolina
water

1. Sift flour and salt together.
2. Put some semolina on the platter and sprinkle on a bit of water. With a flat, circular motion of the hands, gently swish ingredients together, forming little balls of dough.
3. Add some flour and a few more drops of water and keep rubbing and swishing. Keep adding semolina then drops of water then flour, bit by bit, working them in. When both flours have been added, keep flicking in water and rubbing and swishing until many tiny balls form. For an expert this happens quickly; for me it takes about half an hour.
4. When balls are small, throw them into sifter and shake them through onto a large plate or flat basket. Push any remaining balls through in a circular motion with your fist. They will slip through the holes, becoming what looks rewardingly like couscous.
5. If time allows, leave couscous in the sun for a few hours to dry out; if not, steam immediately.

Steamed Couscous

If you don't have a couscousiere, you can use a steamer with a muslin cloth in the top half to prevent the couscous falling through.

rosewater
olive oil
smen (rancid butter) or clarified butter

1. Lightly tip half the couscous into the steamer and fit it over a pot of simmering stock or stew. When the steam starts to come through, add the rest of the couscous on top. Cover tightly and steam for 15 minutes. Fork through the couscous occasionally to keep grains from sticking.
2. Tip couscous out onto a large plate or platter and spread out to cool. Sprinkle a tiny bit of rosewater over it and put a little olive oil on your hands. Rub grains gently with your hands, separating any stuck together, adding a little water to plump it up as you go.
3. Place back in steamer and repeat steps 1 and 2 twice more. Three times in all. On the third time, instead of rubbing in oil, rub in a little butter.

The butter gives it an indescribable creaminess. Now it is ready to eat and is as light and perfumed as a dream. If you are using packet couscous you can still steam it using this method. Wash the couscous (allow about 100 g per person), strain it and let it sit in a flat pan for ten minutes so the grains can swell a bit. Then proceed to steam it three times as above.

Radiga's Couscous Rabbit Stew

Serves 4–6

1 large rabbit, portioned – use the liver and heart
1 medium onion, finely sliced
4 large cloves garlic, halved and with germ removed
1 tbsp olive oil
1 tsp ground ginger
1 tsp smoked paprika
2 star anise
1 tsp ground cumin
1 tsp salt
handful coriander, chopped
1 cup water
350 g carrots, peeled and quartered
350 g little swedes, washed and halved

1. In the lower part of the couscousiere or in a large pot, put meat, onion, garlic, olive oil, spices, herbs and water. Bring to boil, then lower heat to a simmer, covered, for half an hour. Add carrots and swedes.
2. Now commence steaming the fresh couscous. By the time you have finished steaming the couscous, the stew will be perfectly cooked.

Put the steamed couscous on a large serving dish in a mound with a well in the centre. Place the meat in the centre and the vegetables around it. Pour over some cooking juices and serve the rest in a bowl.

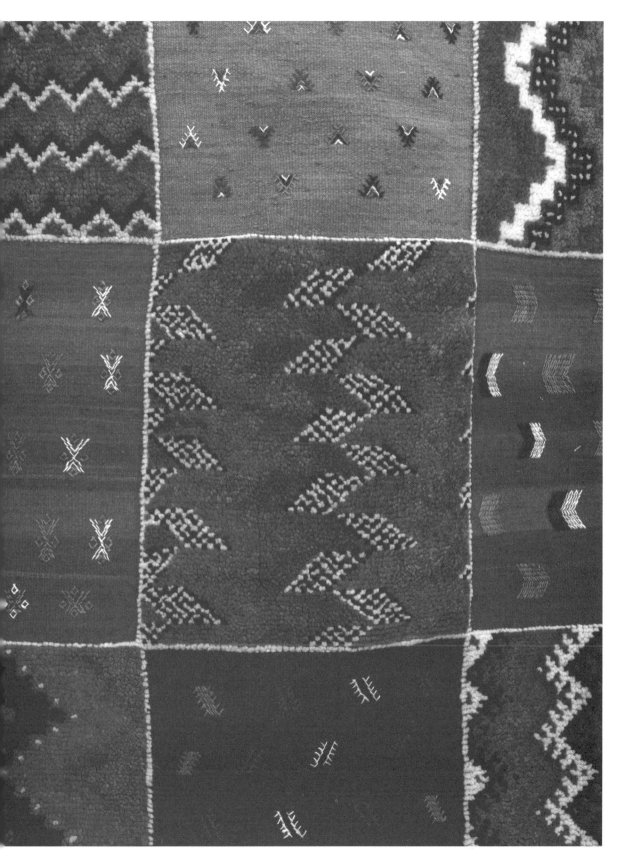

Another way of cooking couscous, one which you will only experience if you eat in a Moroccan home, is the sweet method called seffa. Seffa is a type of couscous that is very fine and made only from semolina and water, no flour. It is quite complicated to make a real seffa, so I have given a simplified recipe here. Cooking the couscous the long way, by triple steaming over boiling water, will produce a superior result, but I am giving you a quick option. Seffa is a very rich palace dish, normally served with an ice-cold drink, such as almond milk or buttermilk. They rub a lot more butter into seffa than a regular couscous.

Seffa
Sweet Couscous

Serves 6

300 g couscous
¼ preserved lemon and 1 tbsp of juice
2 tbsp sugar
freshly ground black pepper
1 tbsp butter or extra virgin olive oil
60 g (½ cup) raisins
50 ml (¼ cup) orange flower water
60 g (½ cup) walnuts
60 g (½ cup) blanched almonds
60 g (½ cup) dates
½ cup mint, chopped
½ tsp cinnamon
icing sugar and cinnamon for decoration
extra dates dipped in sesame seeds for decoration

1. Place couscous in a large bowl. Add preserved lemon juice, sugar, pepper and butter or oil. Rub in with your hands. Pour over just enough boiling water to cover couscous and put aside to 'cook'.
2. Soak raisins in orange flower water for half an hour.
3. Coarsely chop nuts in a food processor and chop up dates. Discard preserved lemon flesh and thinly slice skin.
4. Fluff up couscous with a large fork. Toss in raisins and orange water, nuts, dates, preserved lemon, mint and cinnamon.

Pile couscous in a pointed hill on a serving dish. Sprinkle icing sugar over in a criss-cross pattern and add some cinnamon on top. Decorate edges with sesame rolled dates. Serve warm or at room temperature.

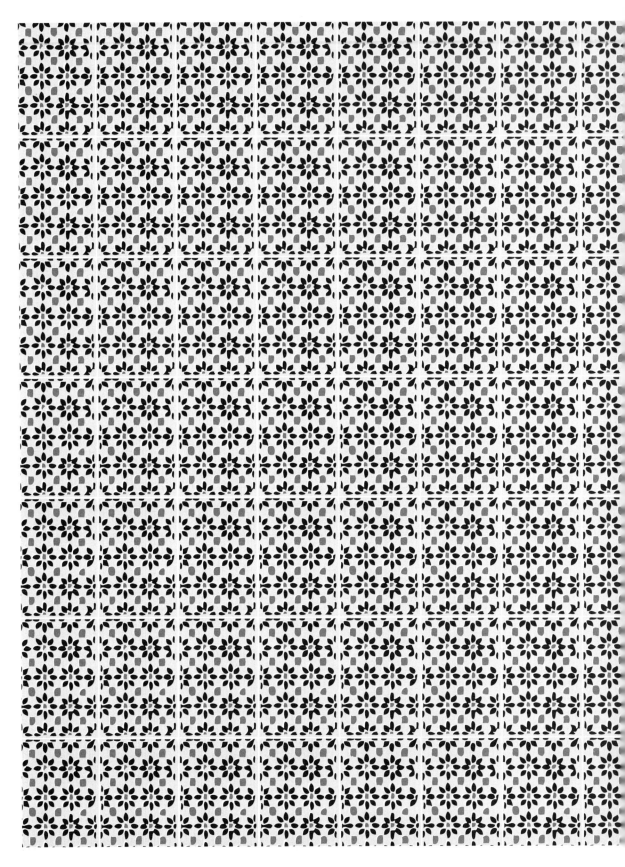

Chapter Three
Tagine & Trid

Being from a crossroad of civilisation, Moroccan food benefits from the influence of many cultures' cuisines. Over the course of history Phoenicians, Arabs, Berbers, Moors, Spaniards, Jews and French people have found their way there and many set up shop. The spice trade from Arabia and across Northern Africa is largely responsible for the soul of Moroccan cooking. Sometimes it seems that Moroccans are in love with every spice in the world and it's true, spices have been part of their cuisine for a very long time. Centuries ago, having access to expensive spices from exotic places meant you were rich so it was a way not only of trading, but also of showing social status. The more spices you had and the more refined your cooking, the more successful you were. The Phoenicians were the first outsiders to enter Morocco and they brought spices with them. The Arabs took to these luxurious spices with enthusiasm and they in turn took them over to Spain, where Christopher Columbus experienced them and decided to establish his own spice route to avoid having to pay so much to the Arabs, who then controlled the trade. But it was actually the Portuguese explorer Vasco da Gama who, in 1498, established a lucrative trade route, figuring out how to sail directly to India via the Cape of Good Hope. This is how the Portuguese discovered that the spices didn't actually come from 'Arabia', as the wily Arabs told them – they came from India, specifically the Kerala Province. The most important spice was pepper, but there were not only spices – the Indians specialised in incense and opium, too. The rest is history, with those spices and drugs changing Europe forever.

The most common spices used in everyday Moroccan cooking are:

Aniseed – warm and liquorice

Black pepper – hot and floral

Coriander seeds – sweet and citrusy

Cinnamon – sweet and woody

Cumin – sweet and aniseedy

Ginger – sweet and peppery

Paprika – hot and smoky

Saffron – pungent and bitter-sweet

Turmeric – earthy and slightly bitter

The peregrine smells of coriander, cinnamon, cumin, ginger, turmeric, paprika, saffron, fenugreek, coriander, pepper, aniseed, dried rosebuds and harissa are all found in the spice souks of Marrakech, particularly Rahba Kedima Square, which is actually triangle-shaped. I love this square because not only does it house spice and magic shops but also the groovy Café des Épices and my favourite hole-in-the-wall lunch restaurant run by a lady called Amina. At no. 152 we interviewed and filmed the very cool Rasta man Rachid in his spice shop – think dreadlocks, wild beard and big knitted hat. Both spice sellers and home cooks will make up their own blends called ras el-hanout, which could be anything from five to a hundred spices all ground up. Apart from all the usual spices, ras el-hanout can also contain 'esoteric' ones like nigella (acid tasting), galangal, ground rosebuds, lavender, ash or rowan berries (astringent tasting and supposedly aphrodisiac), grains of paradise (malagueta pepper), orris root (coffee tasting), mace (essential in ras el-hanout) and chufa or tigernut. What you put in a ras el-hanout depends on what you are cooking but it is strong – you don't need much. You also find other useful products at spice stalls – it's kind of like a local pharmacy. You can buy things like inky-blue indigo for dying fabric, sandalwood and lumps of natural stone alum intended for personal grooming (you wet the stone, it becomes sticky and you use it as aftershave or deodorant).

A Simple Ras el-Hanout

6 cloves
30 g (2 tbsp) black peppercorns
10 dried rosebuds
10 cardamom pods
15 g (1 tbsp) mace
1 tsp aniseed
14 g (1 tbsp) galangal
1 tbsp dried lavender
15 g (1 tbsp) allspice berries

1. Grind all the ingredients together in a spice grinder and keep in a sealed container.

Mountains of dried and fresh **roses** are found in the spice souks all over Morocco and are used in many preparations. Dried rosebuds are part of ras el-hanout, to be used in tagines, meatballs, with game and in couscous stuffings. Rather than being overwhelmed by the powerful spices like turmeric, nutmeg, cardamom and allspice in ras el-hanout, the roses add a musky, haunting flavour. Rose and orange petal water flavour cakes, pastries, desserts, meat dishes, salads, ice creams and sorbets in Morocco. All roses are edible, though some are more appetising than others. You can add rosewater and orange blossom water to poached apples for dessert, sprinkle over grated apples for breakfast and add a dash to a cherry flan. Eating rose-flavoured sweets is like eating summer and romance and longing. When you eat with your fingers, a jug of water scented with rose or orange blossom is poured over the hands before and after the meal. Quite often the first thing served at a meal is a glass of cool rose-perfumed almond milk. Scatter crimson rose petals over the dinner table, in fountains and down the driveway so that when the person of your dreams comes home, they will have soft petals underfoot.

According to Berber women, who have pellucid, pale skin, you should splash your face in rosewater morning and night. Not only does it refresh and moisturise the skin but, like lavender, it is a tranquilliser and anti-depressant. A spray of it will make a busload of hot tourists smell wonderful and it is widely used in beauty preparations. You can also add rosewater to your final hair rinse to prevent hair loss. If you sleep with a bag of dried rosebuds under your pillow, you will have sweet dreams forever and if you add a drop of it to mint tea you will never be sad. Most of the great perfumes are made of roses. The Arabs invented the distilling process centuries ago and their alambic or quettara stills are basically the same as a modern still – it takes three and a half kilograms of rosebuds or orange blossoms to make three and a half litres of fragrant water.

The origins of the rose lie in Central Asia, from where it spread eastward to North America and west to Asia Minor and Europe. No wild rose has ever been discovered in the Southern Hemisphere or south of the equator. The Romans believed that roses rained from the sky at the birth of Venus (Aphrodite to the Greeks) when she emerged from the sea, standing on a scallop shell. Maybe that is why Cleopatra turned up to meet Mark Antony in a golden barge decorated with roses and powered by silver oars and purple sails. She presented herself as Aphrodite, wreathed and garlanded with roses. Roses were also strewn around the palace chambers, couches lined with rose-filled mattresses, rose net bags used as cushions and in the grounds roses even floated on the lakes.

The Romans wore rose wreaths at their banquets. Their drinking cups were hung with roses. A petal was plucked from a wreath and put into the wine before drinking – to toast a friend. Roman writer Pliny believed that rose petals in wine delayed drunkenness. Some Roman orgies were held on carpets of rose petals, and a popular idea after a meal was a cascade of rose petals released from the ceiling. On one occasion, several guests were suffocated to death after being buried beneath a rose avalanche. As a food, the Romans decorated rose puddings with candied rose petals, ate rose jellies, rose honey and rose pâtés. Roman homes and tabletops were scattered with roses. Lovers exchanged rose wreaths. Bathwater had roses put in it to help preserve the skin, and after bathing they massaged each other's bodies with rose ointments.

Roses have always symbolised sex. Yes, I'm sorry, you're not even safe in the garden – why do you think so many middle-aged men grow roses? The rose is an ancient symbol of sensuality, fertility and womanhood. It stands for the universal woman who, as the great goddess, is mother of the world. The Romans worshipped Flora, the goddess of fruit trees, vineyards and flowers and on her special day they gave women roses. The original rose has five petals only, symbolising the five appendages of the body – legs, arms and head. These capture the essentials of life: sex, birth, life and death.

Another staple of the spice souks, although it is not Moroccan but Tunisian, is the tasty chilli paste harissa. Chillis, red capsicums and paprika were brought to North Africa from Goa in India by the Ottoman Turks. The seeds grew really well and wherever they grew, they developed their own distinct flavour – hot, sweet, bitter, mild, smoky. Tunisians eat harissa with everything – salads, soups, couscous, tagines, fish, eggs, bread and kebabs – but Moroccans don't generally like very hot food and prefer their harissa on the side. I love it because the heat is tempered by the sweet flavours of coriander and cumin. You don't usually put it directly on food – it is mixed with a tablespoon of sauce from a couscous, for example, then poured over the meal. Or it is mixed with lemon juice. You can buy it commercially but home-made harissa is much better. Ten years of eating couscous royale and tagines in Paris ensured that I became addicted to this stuff.

Harissa

100 g dried chilli peppers
6 cloves garlic
1 tsp sea salt
2 tbsp coriander seeds
2 tbsp cumin seeds
²/₃ cup extra virgin olive oil

1. With rubber gloves on, cut chillis open and remove seeds and stalk. Soak flesh in hot water for a few minutes.
2. Drain chillis and smash together with the other spices in a pestle and mortar or a food processor.
4. Gradually add olive oil in a stream until well incorporated. Sauce can be smooth or a little chunky.

You don't really need to, but it's probably a good idea to keep this in the fridge.

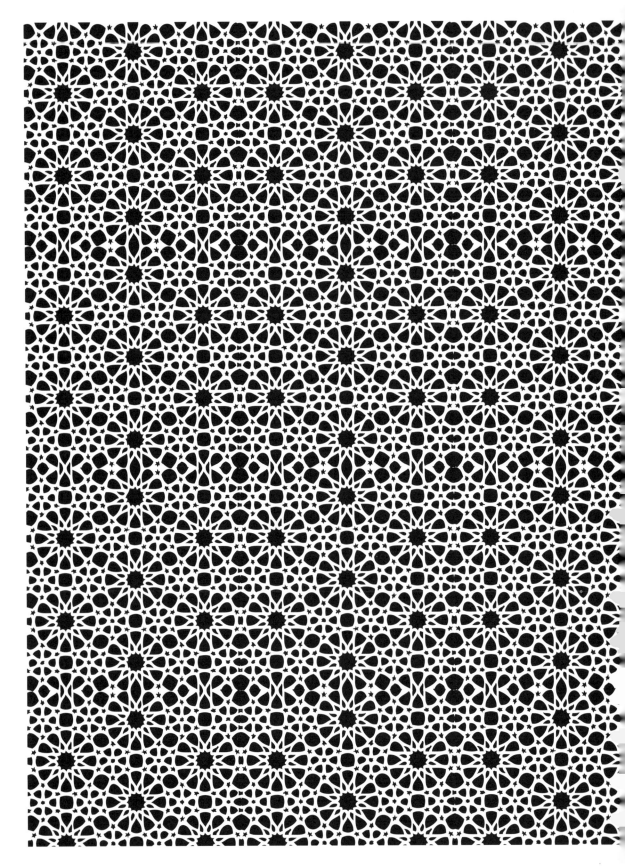

Along with spices there are certain ingredients intrinsic to Moroccan cuisine and one of them is the olive – one of the oldest, most revered foods on the planet and native to the nearby Mediterranean. You will see stands of all sorts of glistening olives throughout Morocco – mountains of them alongside mountains of sun-kissed preserved lemons. You can choose between green ones tossed with enough chilli to send a Pakistani snake charmer into cardiac arrest; big purple ones, which are almost sweet with their addition of preserved lemons, garlic and parsley; black ones cured in salt and laced with thyme; mixtures of olives with sliced oranges and artichokes. The salt-cured olives are one of my favourites. You pick the olives black, therefore very ripe, put them in a big plastic bag with salt and leave them out in the sun for three days. They are quite shrivelled and taste intensely olivey and saline.

Marrakech olives are cured in cellars along the back streets and people come down from the mountains with their own local specialities. These little rarities you have to know about because no two batches are the same. Neighbouring Tunisia grows huge amounts of olives, mostly for export as oil. Morocco grows a lot less and they export little oil, but their cured olives are the best you will ever eat. They are the champions of the world: fabulously healthy, large and smooth. Morocco produces 400,000 tons of olives a year, exports 60,000 tons of eating olives, second only to Spain; it supplies three-quarters of France's olives, many of which are then exported as 'French', and now even supplies Spain. The scandal is that labour is ten times cheaper in

Morocco than in Spain, so it is more cost effective for the Spanish to buy Moroccan olives and onsell them.

Most of Morocco is good olive-growing territory, but it is especially good from the coastal fringe, Meknes, up to the Atlas and Rif Mountains and over to the Sahara. Ninety-nine per cent of Moroccan olive groves (forests really) are picholine or beldi, a hardy wild variety. Green olives, harvested from mid-September through to the end of October, are cracked open with a wooden paddle on the stone ground and soaked in brine and sometimes caustic soda. The violet ones are sliced once with a razor to aid the curing and the black ones remain ripening on the tree until late November or December. They are so ripe the skin will take on the salt water without being broken. The Spanish marinate their olives for much longer than the Moroccans, but the Moroccans say they get very good depth of flavour simply because the olives are naturally and painstakingly cured. As the old saying goes, you get out of something what you put into it.

One day in Fès I found a ramshackle stall selling unfiltered, raw mountain olive oil. One teaspoon of it would have unplugged your arteries for a month. On the road from Fès to Tangier sits a little crossroads city called Ouezzane which, legend has it, produces the best olives in Morocco. Jews fleeing Andalusia in the fifteenth century settled there, and although their descendants have departed, their olive recipes are still used. Tribes in the mountains tend small groves, which are getting smaller with each generation. When a man dies his land is divided between his sons, meaning that over the years the plots have become tiny and uneconomic – and the oil very expensive. This is why you hardly ever see anyone cooking with it – they mostly use peanut or seed oils. I bought a small plastic water bottle of the dark green, thick oil. It tasted strong, had a high acidity, but the Moroccans don't chuck it all over the place like I do; they add a little, like smen or argan oil, to flavour a dish or dip bread in it for breakfast.

Every year a million seedlings are added to Morocco's fifty million olive trees, in part for soil conservation and wind breaks, but mostly for eating olives. Moroccans unfortunately are their own worst enemies in terms of modern cultivation and marketing. They are an ancient people and they like doing things the way they've always been done, which basically means they persist with medieval methods. They've got cellphones and better roads but sanitary standards are slack and delivery attitudes are mañana mañana, which of course drives potential markets like the USA nuts. Instead of protecting against a drought they say, 'It doesn't matter whether it rains or not. The trees don't care – they just keep growing. It is their job to grow and our job to pick.' They leave the trees exactly how they've been for generations, without pruning, and when the trees get too high to bang the olives down, they just get longer sticks or have the kids climb up. Regarding the oil, a small number of large olive mills produce very good extra virgin oil but in fairly primitive conditions. They are pressed in small, old-style mat presses, with donkeys or camels powering the grinding stones. According to my friends at Riad Fès, the best olive oil in Morocco is Primanova, pressed by Les Conserves de Meknes, and each bottle is numbered. It is strong and dark – exactly how they like it. This is the one to buy if you want to take home Moroccan olive oil.

Marinade for Olives

6 tbsp flat leaf parsley, chopped
6 tbsp coriander, chopped
2 cloves garlic, chopped
½ tsp hot red pepper flakes
¼ tsp ground cumin
4–6 tbsp extra virgin olive oil
lemon juice to taste
500 g olives of your choice

1. Combine all ingredients and leave to marinate for at least 24 hours.

Olives with Orange Blossom Water and Artichokes

½ cup orange blossom water
1 dried chilli pepper, chopped
1 tsp sea salt
6 tbsp extra virgin olive oil
500 g olives of your choice
200 g artichoke hearts (better if fresh)
1 orange, sliced with skin on

1. Combine all ingredients except artichokes and orange slices and marinate for at least 24 hours.
2. Toss in quartered artichoke hearts and serve orange slices on the side.

I mentioned preserved lemons earlier – another intrinsic and truly, deeply, madly fabulous ingredient which I will use in almost anything (I even put a little in my Christmas cake instead of candied peel – try it). Moroccans normally use preserved lemons in salads and tagines. They are silky and plump and completely unmistakeable – you cannot replace the intense, salty-acidy, piquant taste with a fresh lemon. The best way to never run out of them is to preserve them yourself. It's dead easy – you just have to think of it in advance. You can't make too many jars because they last for years and years unopened. In Morocco they use doqq and boussera lemons; at home, choose the most acid lemons you can. In Safi, because of the Jewish influence, they put in a cinnamon stick, cloves, coriander seeds, peppercorns and a bay leaf.

Preserved Lemons

2 kg thick-skinned, acidy lemons
2 x 1-litre preserving jars
300 g salt
water or lemon juice

1. Scrub the lemons with a hard brush.
2. With a sharp knife, cut each lemon lengthwise, stopping 1.5 cm before the bottom to keep the halves attached. Turn lemon upside down and rotate to cross-cut it in half lengthwise on the other side, again stopping 1.5 cm before the bottom.
3. Sterilise the jars in boiling water for 10 minutes.
4. Hold lemons open by squeezing gently and stuff both ends with salt. Close them with your hand and pack in the jars as you go.
5. When jars are full, press lemons down well and sprinkle over salt. Fill jar almost to the top with boiling water or lemon juice. Seal jars.
6. Leave the jars of lemons in a cool place to steep for at least three weeks. A white film may form on top – it's natural and is washed off. What happens to transform the lemons is that they release their oily juice, which mingles with the salt and produces a honey-thick, unctuous syrup. Don't discard it – use it in salad dressings and to flavour tagines and other stews.

To use a preserved lemon, remove it from the jar and rinse well in running water. Slide the pulp off with your thumb and discard it – it is rarely used in Moroccan cooking, except sometimes as extra flavour in a tagine. Cut the peel into thick strips and use in tagines of fish, chicken or lamb. It is also added to salads or relishes. The jar of lemons must be refrigerated once open.

Lamb Tagine with Fennel, Preserved Lemons and Artichokes

Serves 6 people

6 large fresh artichokes or 12 tinned hearts, well drained
3 fennel bulbs
3 generous pinches of saffron
1 preserved lemon
1.5 kg lamb shoulder
1 tsp sea salt
freshly ground black pepper
1 tsp ground ginger
1 cinnamon stick
4 cloves garlic, smashed

1. Remove outer leaves of the artichokes and scoop out choke, leaving the hearts. As you go, plunge them immediately into lemon water to prevent browning.
2. Trim fronds (save them) off the fennel then wash, quarter and core. Pop them into the lemon water with the artichokes.
3. Prepare saffron by soaking in ¼ cup of boiling water for 15 minutes.
4. Remove flesh from the preserved lemon and discard it. Rinse peel and cut it into strips.
5. Preheat oven to 180 °C (355 °F). Cut meat into large chunks then place in the tagine dish base. If you don't have a tagine, use a regular casserole dish or clay pot.
6. On top of meat put salt, pepper, ginger, cinnamon stick, garlic, saffron with its juice, preserved lemon strips and ¼ cup of water. Mix them around with your hands. Cover with tagine lid and cook in the oven for one hour.
7. Remove the tagine from oven and add artichokes and fennel, mixing them in with the meat sauce. Put back in oven and continue cooking for half an hour.
8. Serve immediately, bringing the tagine dish to the table. Garnish with chopped fennel fronds and eat with Moroccan bread.

This dish can also be cooked in a heavy-based pot or tagine on top of the stove.

When you mix together spices, olives and preserved lemons, what frequently results is a tagine. The word tagine refers to both the earthenware vessel and its contents. There are as many tagine recipes as there are villages in Morocco. When you are shopping in Morocco you should buy one cheap, unglazed, earthenware tagine for cooking and one ornate, glazed, decorated one for serving on the table. Tagines range in size from single serving to gigantic wedding banquet size. The cooking ones are cheap and unbelievably resilient – you can cook them on a naked flame, on a flat element and in the oven. The stew is placed on the shallow base of the tagine and covered with a pointy lid that has a thick lip at the top to make it easy to remove. Most Moroccan housewives actually cook tagines in pressure cookers then serve them in a decorative tagine dish. They also use the base of the tagine dish to fry fish and they store bread under the conical lid. A French friend told me tagines are very good ice containers.

A tagine is an all-in-one dish and is not normally served with couscous – the starch you eat with it is bread. However, I have noticed over the past few years that restaurants serve a plate of couscous on the side – this is the effect of European taste, I would think. If they can, most Moroccan people come home for a cooked lunch, which is the main meal of the day. The first tagine I ate in Morocco was Djej Emshmel, the most famous one – chicken, olives and preserved lemons. Cooked by Zohra in Kenitra, it comprised of two whole, bright yellow chickens cooked until falling apart with preserved lemons and her home-cured green olives. The bright yellow unfortunately comes from food colouring (it's much better to use real saffron if you can); the other ingredients were ginger, garlic and smen, which is also called beurre rance, which sounds ghastly but tastes delicious when added to cooking. Zohra's olives were crushed, soaked in frequently changed water for eight days, then marinated in brine.

Before you sit down to eat a meal in Morocco, you wash your hands. The tagine platter is placed in the middle of the round table and everyone reaches into the meal, grabbing pieces of chicken and olives with their fingers and using bread to soak up the juices. It is only when you start eating a tagine with your fingers that you understand why it has to be cooked to falling apart – it makes it much easier to grab bits from a whole bird. You use only the first three fingers of your right hand, never the left, and put bits on a small plate in front of you. I was sitting next to Zohra and she kept digging out morsels she observed I liked – such as liver, skin, dark meat and preserved lemon – and putting them on my plate. I was very moved by this intimate bird-feeding. No one had ever picked out food with their own hands and given it to me in my life. (Well, my mother must have but I don't remember.) You put your bones and scraps in little piles on the paper tablecloth in front of you. Everyone washes their hands – at the end you may lick or clean your fingers with serviettes. It is considered very gross to lick your fingers throughout the meal. After the meal you wrap up the paper tablecloth and throw it away, revealing the nice clean one underneath.

Chicken Tagine with Preserved Lemons and Olives

Serves 6

For the marinade or chermoula:
1 cup flat leaf parsley, chopped
1 cup fresh mint, chopped
1 preserved lemon
4 cloves garlic, crushed
2 tsp paprika
2 tsp ground cumin
1 tsp ground ginger
½ tsp salt
2 generous pinches saffron, soaked for half and hour in
    2 tbsp boiling water

1. Place the parsley, mint, flesh of the preserved lemon and garlic in the food processor and blend.
2. Place this paste in a bowl and add the spices, including the saffron water.

For the tagine:
1 large, organic or free range chicken
300 g ripe, acid-free or Roma tomatoes
300 g waxy potatoes
3 tbsp olive oil
125 g purple or green olives
mint and parsley sprigs for garnish

1 Cut chicken into six portions and rub chermoula all over these.
2. Peel and quarter tomatoes. Peel and slice potatoes and slice preserved lemon skin left over from the marinade ingredients.
3. Lay potatoes on the bottom of the tagine or oven dish and then the chicken covered in chermoula. Next, lay down the preserved lemon and lastly the tomatoes.
4. Create a pyramid shape. Pour over olive oil and cover with tagine lid.
5. Bake at 180 °C (355 °F) or simmer on the stove top for half an hour. Add the olives and cook for another 15 minutes.

Place the tagine dish on the table for people to serve themselves. Garnish with sprigs of mint and parsley.

In cheap, open restaurants all over Marrakech you will see pre-made tagines on charcoal braziers, begging you to lift the lid and have a sniff. They are very beautiful and are made from fish, beef, chicken or lamb with vegetables. The food is piled up in a pyramid shape, not just thrown in any old how. You choose your tagine, sit down, get a Coke and watch the telly, eating with your hands – there is no happier way to pass half an hour with your starving friends. Moroccans also eat with a dessert spoon, which I find more manageable but less fun. Afterwards, you are served mint tea. I always ask for a gin and tonic or a glass of wine, which the staff are kind enough to laugh at. When they see me coming in my neighbourhood, they call out, 'Madame Peta, we have the gin out the back', which I am always kind enough to laugh at. Note: you can get alcohol in up-market restaurants.

One day Radiga made us a lamb and prune tagine for lunch. It wasn't part of our course, but everyone wanted the recipe, so here it is. You could also make this with beef.

Lamb and Prune Tagine

Serves 6

1.5 kg lamb leg or shoulder cut into large pieces
1 medium onion, grated
4 large cloves garlic, chopped
1 tsp freshly ground black pepper
1 tsp sea salt
1 tsp paprika
2 star anise
2 tsp ground cumin
4 tbsp olive oil
2 tbsp rich dark honey
½ tsp powdered cinnamon
200 g soaked prunes
50 g blanched almonds
1 tbsp toasted sesame seeds

1. Mix lamb, onion, garlic, pepper, sea salt, paprika, star anise, cumin and olive oil together in a tagine dish and add ½ cup water. Bring to the boil, reduce to a simmer and cover with the tagine lid. Cook for an hour and a half or until lamb is very tender. Add more water from time to time if necessary (it probably won't be as the tagine lid collects moisture). Sauce should be thick, spicy and caramelised.
2. Add honey, cinnamon and prunes and mix in well. Cook for another 10 minutes.
3. Fry almonds in a dash of oil until golden, then chop.

Serve in the tagine dish on the table and garnish with almonds and sesame seeds. Eat with Moroccan bread.

The first time I visited a food market in
Morocco, I found mountains of olives, eggs,
birds in cages, snails, preserved lemons, fresh
coriander and mint, beans, grains, short fat
okra, tomatoes, chickpeas, raisins, hanging
meat and cows' hooves all lined up. The
latter are made into a reputedly delicious dish
called kaariine. Whenever I mentioned this
dish to people, their eyes rolled heavenwards
in ecstasy. At the markets I would wander
around, bumping into donkeys and drinking
mint tea, or just sitting, watching and inhaling the grandeur that is any
souk in Morocco. I discovered there a very thick lamb liver sausage
resembling a giant black pudding and sold in fat slices. I also discovered
khli', salted, marinated strips of dried beef, cooked for a long time
in fat and then preserved in it. It sits in the marinade for a day and is
hung out in the air for ten days until it looks like a mummy's tongue.
This is then cooked in fat, oil, the marinade and water until the water
evaporates. Jars or buckets are filled with layers of meat and fat, and
when you see it in the souk it is usually sticking straight up in its fat,
like black trees in a petrified snow forest. Khli' is deliciously strong,
rich and soft once it has been reheated and added to tagines and soups.
Next to these was a lovely line-up of skinned goats' and sheep's heads,
and brown, undulating tripe.

City markets are fabulous but it is a mistake to spend all your
time in Moroccan cities and not get out into the bled to visit some of
the wild country souks – ten times wilder than anything in a city. On
my first visit to Morocco on yet another azure, rose-scented morning,

a friend and I decided to hire a taxi to take us up to Chefchaouen for the day. Just to get out of Tangier was a performance, as the police are most vigilant. Our driver, Mohamed, had to register himself with his licence and us with our passports before the police would let us leave town. On the road to the Rif Mountains we often saw trucks and cars stopped by police on the side of the road. They were usually looking for kef (marijuana) and the fines are huge, which seems really absurd to me, considering it's one of their biggest cash crops. We came across a market in the dusty village of Amani Hassan, which was the most extraordinary experience. Like travellers from a time machine we wandered into another century, secure in the knowledge that not many tourists would ever come to a market like this one – excepting ours, there were no non-Moroccan faces there. Moroccans are good-looking, fine-boned people, but Riffians are absolutely stunning. These are the real Berbers and original inhabitants of Morocco, still living in a very traditional, ritualised way.

The Riffian mode of transport is donkey and horse, and they are much more respectful of animals than their medina counterparts. The animals were shining, clean and well fed, with beautiful rugs and saddles on their backs and colourful baskets hanging off each side. When you first get to Morocco you want to save every donkey, mule and horse you see, and think the worst thing you could be born as would be a donkey in Morocco. It is true that they are shockingly cruel to animals, especially beasts of burden. The donkeys are very badly cared for, beaten mercilessly and work all day carrying loads three times their poor little body weight. They have abrasions and cuts, are skinny and have rubber tyres on their hooves to grip more easily in the steep, narrow medina streets. This is not to help their legs, some of which literally wobble and look about to break with pain and weight.

Riffian women's attire is famously flamboyant, many-layered and identical – they all wear the same thing with only minor variations, one of them being flowery nighties as part of the layers. First, there is a long-sleeved, mid-calf-length white or pale flowery dress, under which are long white leggings, socks and shoes. Around the waist is the money pouch, then a fouta or red-and-white-striped cotton blanket made of wool in the winter (which is desperately cold) and cotton in the summer. This is wrapped around the waist and attached with ornate silver belts. A striped towel is worn over the head, like a veil falling around the shoulders, and is held on with a tall, wide-brimmed hat decorated with navy-blue pompoms and braids. Keep in mind the morning temperature was 40 °C and rising. Unbelievable that they could wear all these clothes in that heat, but they moved slowly and kept to the shade. Their faces of exquisite beauty are soft and unlined, in spite of the hard physical work they do all day on the farms. They greet each other by kissing hands. Any attempt to photograph these women face on is met with angry rebuff from the men and a quiet turning away from the women. I was told that the ancient Jews used magic to take people's minds by drawing their faces, and to this day Riffians believe the taking of your image by a camera is for the purposes of magic.

It was a very busy, noisy, colourful market with mountain music playing, women carrying babies on their backs in yet another blanket, men holding hands, hens squawking all over the place, raw meat hanging out in the dust and heat, melons, red potatoes, mountains of red onions, olives, grapes, huge tomatoes and vertical gardens of fresh coriander. There were fabulous woven baskets in myriad colours and medicinal shops laid out on the ground in beautifully patterned symmetry, showing off mysterious spices, herbs, bits of dried animals and knowledge in the form of stories and handed-down wisdom.

One side of the market was lined with wild west shops and little cafés reminiscent of Mexico or southern Spain, but the best part of this bazaar was the animal auction with its sleek, healthy horses expertly cared for, sheep with curly horns, goats with silky hair from which Riffians make soft fabric to wrap around themselves, solid handsome cows and proud, staunch farmers in traditional dress. Riffians must be horrified when they see the way animals are treated in the cities.

We dragged ourselves away, but only because we had to get into the air-conditioning of the taxi. My body seemed to be lacking in energy and seriously overheating as water and electrolytes haemorrhaged out of every pore. That combined with crippling diarrhoea, an insatiable thirst for anything sweet and the scandalous realisation that I wasn't as intrepid as I thought I was made me feel quite ill. We drank litres of fresh pure orange juice, never feeling full, until our stomachs were bloated. When we got home we found out it had been 52 °C that day.

Needless to say, as soon as Florence told me about the Tuesday souk near her at Ait Ourir, David and I were in there like pirates. This souk is absolutely, terrifyingly authentic, just like the Amani Hassan one but the folk don't dress up like the Riffians. It is huge and dusty with hundreds of people and many areas specialising in different things – meat, birds, clothes, a whole line of barbers doing shaves, vegetables and fruit, sheep, donkey, horse and camel sales, a donkey carpark and so on. There is a kitchen utensils section, a Berber sauna section, an iron-mongers section and a mechoui section, where they do mechoui differently from how you see it done in Marrakech. The clay pit sits on the surface of the ground, rather than below it. We even saw our favourite gold-toothed lady musician there in her other guise as bread seller.

The meat section is horrific: carcasses, skins and innards lie on the path you are supposed to be walking on. The path was a river of blood and I was glad I wore my inappropriate Robert Clergerie platforms. Stylish David nearly died as his sandals and pale linen pants soaked it all up. Some of our clients were vegetarian, so I warned them in advance. But to their credit, everyone was determined to 'do' the souk in all its magnificent entirety. It's not just that the carcasses are on display – that's okay – it's that the actual killing goes on just in behind them and if you wander in there you would be forgiven for thinking you were in hell. Fortunately, we had Mohamed (now a local celebrity) walking with us holding a sign with his name on it in Arabic. Very easy to get separated from your group in a heaving souk.

We had a far more genteel scene awaiting us when we got home to Dar Tasmayoun – beautiful, calm Radiga and her niece Fátima in the kitchen, prepping to teach us one of my favourite Moroccan dishes, chicken trid. I discovered trid at Dar Mima restaurant in Marrakech – it is said to be the prophet's preferred dish and is sometimes called poor man's pastilla. It seems to be served in differing ways depending on the cook and the region. In Fès the pastry is left whole and in Safi it is torn into pieces. Some cooks serve trid already put together as a composite dish in layers. This one was served in separate parts of meltingly cooked chicken portions, pieces of steamed trid pastry (similar to warka) and a bowl of broth. To eat it you just kept adding the ingredients to the main dish until you were satiated. The origins of this dish are interesting – dried pasta may have first been concocted by the Arabs as a method of preserving flour for the long wanderings across the desert. There is an Arabic recipe in southern Italy called Ciceri e Tria involving chickpeas, strips of pasta and a vegetable broth. Add saffron and chicken, and it becomes the marvellous trid. The dadas (white-clad lady cooks) at Dar Mima make it by marinating chicken pieces in chermoula – a mixture of garlic, onion, cinnamon, ginger, saffron, parsley, coriander and smen – for two hours at least. They then place the chicken and marinade in a pot with six cups of water, bring it to the boil, reduce to a simmer and cook for an hour. Next, they remove chicken from the pot, and keep it warm. They then strain the stock into a saucepan and reduce by hard boiling to about one and a half cups. Finally, they reheat the torn trid or spring roll pastry in a steamer so it is flaccid, not crispy, and pile it onto a plate. They serve the chicken on another plate and the sauce in a bowl.

Radiga actually made our trid from guinea hens – the stew itself is simple but the interesting part is making the trid pastry, which requires a different method from warka. Moroccans usually use chicken but they also make it with merguez, meatballs and beef. In fact, you can make it with anything you like. The three parts are the trid pastry, the sauce and the meat. The gastronomads really enjoyed this class because Radiga showed us that trid pastry is achievable and all you need is asbestos fingertips. They were thrilled at the delicious crispy pastry sheets and dismayed when I said they were going to get dunked and lose all their crispiness. However, when they sat down to the finished product, they discovered how good this dish is. It is, in fact, like having pasta with a wet sauce.

Chicken Trid

Serves 6

For the trid pastry:
500 g flour
1 tsp salt
warm water in a small bowl
olive oil in a bowl for working the dough

1. Put flour on the bench and make a well in the centre. Into the well put salt and ½ cup of water. Work flour and water together to form a wet dough. You may need to add more water. Knead for 5 minutes, then rest for 5 minutes covered in cling film. Moroccans do this in a large, flat plate to which the dough doesn't seem to stick.
2. Either use a shallow-sided, medium-sized Teflon frying-pan right-side up, or turn a frying-pan upside down, directly onto medium heat.
3. Pinch dough into little balls. Dip your fingers into the oil and press each ball out into very thin discs the size of the frying-pan. It doesn't matter if it gets holes and you should be able to almost see through it.

As you make each disc, pick it up with your fingertips and place it onto the frying-pan on a medium heat.

4. Turn each disc over after a minute. Keep doing this for a few minutes until golden and quite crisp. Remove from heat and place on a plate.
5. Tear all the cooked discs of dough into big pieces and set aside until you are ready to serve the rest of the meal.

Chermoula marinade:
1 small red onion, finely chopped
1 tbsp freshly ground black pepper
2 generous pinches of saffron
2 tsp ground ginger
1 tsp sea salt
2 tbsp olive oil
2 tbsp water
1 tbsp smen (rancid butter) or butter
2 tbsp flat leaf parsley, chopped
2 tbsp coriander, chopped

For the chicken and sauce:
1 large organic or free range chicken including the liver, portioned
1 large red onion, chopped
1 preserved lemon, sliced

1. Mix together all chermoula ingredients. Rub chicken with the chermoula and marinate for about an hour.
2. Place chicken and marinade in a large pot. Add onions and preserved lemon and a cup of water. Bring to the boil, turn down to a simmer and cover. Cook for 45 minutes. Taste for seasoning. There should be lots of sauce.

Warm up the trid pastry in the oven and arrange on a serving platter. Place the chicken on top and pour some of the sauce over. Serve the rest of the sauce in a bowl. Some people also serve the pastry, chicken and sauce in separate dishes and put it together themselves.

Florence has pomegranate trees all over her property. According to legend the beautiful, ancient pomegranate was fertilised by a drop of water from paradise. Moroccans say you should eat this fruit with the flesh as this tans the stomach, and each seed that is found in a person's stomach lights up his heart and silences the whispering devil for forty days. It was once a symbol of fertility (all those seeds); then in Christian times it became symbolic of the oneness of the universe. The Arabs used it to flavour meat dishes and make drinks like sorbets from the snow in the mountains. It's quite an effort to eat a pomegranate as each little red seed has to be dug out and then the pip spat out (or not), but the taste is sublimely sweet and sour and the seeds sort of burst in your mouth. You can sprinkle them on salads, ice cream and tagines. There is a tasty chicken tagine in which you make a paste from pomegranate juice (I use pomegranate molasses), cumin, cloves, peppercorns, nutmeg, cinnamon, salt and garlic then marinate the chicken in it, and finally cook in the tagine dish with a little stock. I've also used pomegranate molasses in desserts, for example a fig and pomegranate tart. You can obtain the fresh juice by breaking down the seeds in a food processor then straining the juice out. Moroccans quite often eat them for breakfast with diced apples and rosewater. I think it would be delicious with lamb, which is the way the Moors would have used it in place of honey. To this end I have composed a recipe for pomegranates and yoghurt, which goes perfectly with the keftas in Chapter One.

Pomegranate and Yoghurt Dip

Makes 2 cups

300 ml (1½ cups) thick Greek-style yoghurt
garlic clove, finely minced
seeds of 1 pomegranate
¹/₃ cup mint or coriander, chopped
sea salt and freshly ground black pepper to taste

1. Mix all ingredients together.

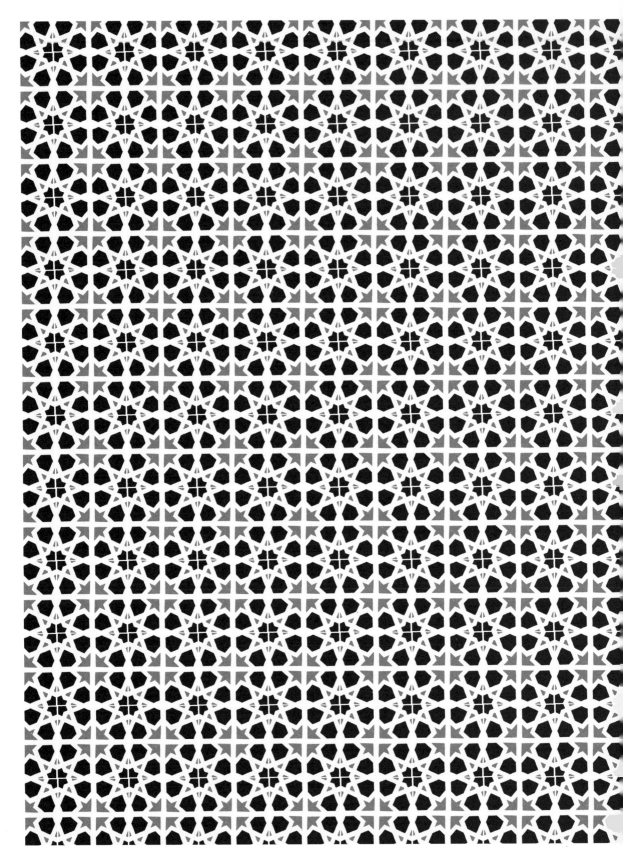

Chapter Four
Bread & Sweets

Moroccan houses are built differently from Western ones, mostly because of the climate and the excessive hospitality they like to indulge in. The first house I entered in Morocco was in Kenitra on the coast – it was a relatively modern, suburban house with a garden. On the doorstep of the large, one-storey dwelling I removed my shoes and was welcomed with handshakes and two kisses by Mohamed and Zohra Bouhdoud. They said I could also call them Haji and Haja, the names given to all devout Muslims who have made the pilgrimage to Mecca. Achieving this pilgrimage in their middle age, given the long distance travelled, was clearly the pinnacle of their lives and they referred proudly to enlarged photos of themselves, dressed in white at Mecca. Straight ahead was the small kitchen, and on either side of the foyer two large rooms, one a formal lounge with chandeliers, lace curtains over white shutters, red satin door curtains swept up, red brocade coverings on the banquettes, and a photo of the King in a jellaba. The other was similar but less formal. In this room they ate and watched television. I went straight into the blue-tiled, white-walled kitchen where I could smell coriander being chopped up. Here, Zohra and her maid were preparing whole sea bream, which they had chopped into three, bones, head and all. These they rubbed in thum (garlic), kahmoon (cumin), falfla hamra (paprika) and fresh qesbur (coriander), then fried in huge amounts of vegetable oil. On the side they were frying chips or tships as they call them, which they love in Morocco – the greasier the better. We sat down outside in the garden and the maid brought out the fish, tships, green salad and bread.

The second house I stayed in was with Latifa Borki (née Bouhdoud). The family was full of generosity, jokes, questions and warmth. It's no big deal to them to have visitors: they give and expect to receive open-handed hospitality as a way of life. Even if your being there is inconvenient, they will never admit it. The children showed not the slightest sign of resentment at losing their room and referred to it as my room, asking permission to enter when they needed something or wanted to visit. I would get up in the morning and sometimes find other children who had stayed the night, and the day I left they gave their house to a visiting family to stay in. To give you an idea of how important hospitality is to Moroccans, the Borkis have three living rooms: one downstairs with Moroccan-style banquettes, another more formal one upstairs, and a European-style one which is also upstairs. Like all Moroccans, Latifa and her husband Hicham adore their children, indulging them, cuddling them, playing with them and talking with them all day.

One day they decided to take me to visit Hicham's sister Nadia in the blue fishing town of Larache, up the coast towards Tangiers. It is called blue because all the doors and shutters on the whitewashed buildings are the most beautiful Andalusian blue; all taxis are the same blue and the sky is only slightly paler. I liked the look of this tranquil town with its Hispano-Moorish arches, old town walls built by the Portuguese in the sixteenth century and relaxed atmosphere – much prettier than French-built Kenitra. It was up the coast at Portuguese-held Asilah that in 1578 the Portuguese launched the disastrous crusade which resulted in the death of Sebastian I, King of Portugal, and the passing of Portugal and its Moroccan territories to Spain. Nadia's modern house on Rue Ibn Khaldoun was on three levels and she welcomed us at the ground level after we had leaned on the intercom. Following much kissing and hand shaking, we went upstairs to the first floor. It was early evening, around 7.30 p.m., so time for le goûter or afternoon tea. While we were waiting for it to be prepared, we lay around on banquettes, chatting and extolling the virtues of lying around. We were in the grand salon – a very large, opulent room with shuttered windows that looked out onto the square. Sumptuous embossed velour in maroon, pink and blue covered the banquettes; thick ornate carpets were spread on the marble floor and chandeliers sparkled from the ceiling. Two large, eight-sided inlaid tables and ten little ones graced the room. The only art on the walls was a painting of Nadia's husband. But what walls! The top third and ceiling was hand-crafted white stucco muqarna work, and the lower two thirds, the famous geometrical zellij tiles. They had been treated so they shone at night.

A leftover from the Spanish past is that lovely pastime found in both Italy and Spain the passeggiata, in Morocco abbreviated to passa: the evening stroll between 6 and 9 p.m. The heart of it all in Larache is Place de la Liberation (which used to be known as Plaza de España), a good example of colonial Spanish design. Everyone comes out onto the street, some dressed up, some not, to walk up and down, check out the opposite sex, have a smoke and a tea or beer, play cards, gossip and relax. Moroccans are very good at relaxing; in fact, they are very good at just doing nothing. This is the time when people have secret rendezvous, borrow the family car without anyone knowing and have snacks at the stalls along the port. Then you make your way home to dinner, which in Nadia's house that night was served at 10.45 p.m.

I took myself on a tour of the large house and discovered on the first floor a modern kitchen, four bedrooms, bathroom and a living room with television. Up on the second floor was another kitchen, shower and more multi-purpose rooms, apparently for the servants. On the roof was a third kitchen and terrace overlooking the town, and up the stairs to a fourth level was the clothes line and wash tubs. The house kitchens were used for prep, but Nadia preferred the cooks to do their frying and stewing on the roof because of the odour. Dinner was the regulation salad of diced tomatoes, onions and capsicum, bowls of olives, deep-fried shrimp, the adored stone-cold tships, crumbed fried sole, home-made bread and pasta (with ketchup on top!). I started counting all the people, including the servants, and looked around the gorgeous salon with a growing horror of realisation that this was not only where I was going to sleep (on banquettes with bullet-proof cushions), but that Latifa and the family would also be joining me.

My worst nightmare, apart from having to share a hotel room, is a communal-sleeping, native-style, Moroccan-camping, boarding-school pyjama party! I knew it would have been unforgivable to look for a hotel, so braced myself for yet another sleepless night. I had hardly slept since I had been in Morocco as it was all communal. I am used to the shrunken, gritty-eyed, irritable walking death of insomnia but I could get sick of it one day and flip. I swallowed hysteria and watched as the servants (always silent, always unacknowledged) brought in armfuls of sheets and blankets and the palace was transformed into a hospital ward. I waited in the dark for the night nurse to do her round of sedatives but my dreams went unanswered. When I woke up in the morning, I saw people in the house I hadn't seen before – old men, young boys, children. I went for another recce to solve the mystery and spied lots of rugs hanging over the low walls of the roof. This is where they all slept – on the roof on rugs. More Moroccan tent parties.

Medina homes or riads are not built to show off to the neighbours. According to Islam, family and God are much more important than displaying wealth. In the West it's the opposite – we let everyone know where we're at by the exterior of our houses. Inside the pink walls of the Marrakech medina are all the flat-topped, courtyard houses. Looked at from above, the city resembles a beehive or maze – confusing, complicated and impenetrable. If you're on the ground it is even harder – for riads deep in the medina, you practically have to take a ball of string or leave a trail of breadcrumbs to get home. The upside is that there is always some kid who knows exactly where you are going (for a few dirhams). All you see of a riad from the outside is a tall, boring wall and a small door, sometimes coloured brightly, sometimes with Fatima's hand as a door knocker. Fátima was the prophet's daughter and she wards off evil – insha'Allah, if God wills it.

There's a lot of insha'Allah in Morocco. It's kind of a fatalistic sigh which means 'I have no control over anything' – it is all in the hands of God. If I have asked the taxi to turn up at 5.30 p.m., it will only happen if God wills it. This attachment to God and his capriciousness sets in at a very young age. One day I sat in on a tiny school for preschoolers while religious instruction was going on. Islam shares its roots with the monotheistic faiths which sprang from the Middle East – Christianity and Judaism – but is much younger than both of those. Islam in Morocco is interesting because the indigenous culture is Berber, which accounts for 80 per cent of the people. Berbers are Hamites with a bit of Nordic, among other things, mixed in, which may account for their fairness and blue eyes. In the seventeenth century the Arabs swept in and everyone embraced Islam, so although a Moroccan may proclaim: 'I am not Arab, I am Berber', they are all united by a common religion.

The little creatures I saw at the preschool were reciting and clapping and singing the Koran to the best of their ability, some bored and falling off their stools, some giggling, some pinching each other, and one little girl was a sure candidate to replace the major domo at the Paris hammam. She sat very straight with her fists clenched, a ferocious look on her face and chanted at the top of her voice. Next step will be the peroxide – God help her husband. I had to tip the teacher to let me watch this, which showed me that nothing is for free in Morocco, not even watching children pray.

The word riad comes from the Arabian word for garden, ryad, and the structure is an adaptation of a Roman villa. The house is built all around a geometrically precise central courtyard and the interior is open to the sky. Some riads have a canvas curtain on the roof which can be pulled across if it rains. The ground floor comprises a central courtyard garden in four squares with a fountain in the middle. There will be rooms off it like the kitchen, storage rooms, the bathroom and various salon-type spaces. Stairs lead up to the first floor, which has a patio going most of the way round. This floor will have cloister-type bedrooms with windows, not to the outside but looking onto the interior, a bathroom and one or more salons. The top level is flat and lots goes on up there: cooking, hanging out the washing, spying on other people's houses and gossiping. It's a place for women – men and visitors are generally not welcome.

Riads can be small and humble or they can be huge palaces. Riad Fès is an example of the latter. Walking into this lofty, refurbished palace was like walking into *One Thousand and One Nights*. The owners have resurrected it from ruin to its former inspirational beauty. The architecture is a fine example of the Andalusian Moroccan style, resplendent with ornate patios, a tiled panoramic roof with restaurant, swimming pool, solarium, lavishly furnished bedrooms, hot tubs and hammam. The ornamental muqarna plaster work, zellij mosaic tiles, tadelakt, hand-rubbed plaster finishing and carved and painted wood have been patiently preserved, and outside are richly planted gardens with pavilions and elaborate tiles. The garden in Muslim cultures is symbolic of the beauty of creation and therefore a reflection of God. The aim is to create harmony through a combination of scent and colour so there are plants, tinkling fountains and birds singing. Fruit, laurel and cypress trees provide shade, and jasmine, rose and geranium flowers pleasure the nose.

Our hotel, the Hôtel du Trésor in the Riad Zitoun area of the medina, was bought by interior decorator extraordinaire, Adriano Pirani, in 2007 and restored by him. The first time David and I saw this hotel we fell hopelessly in love with it and stopped looking elsewhere for accommodation at that very moment. It had only just opened and not many people knew about it. Original Moroccan tiles frame a courtyard graced with an ancient orange tree and cooling little swimming pool. The pool is framed with heavy white curtains, creating an air of mystery and calm in stark contrast to the madly, busily tiled staircase and office. Every one of the thirteen rooms is by luxury hotel standards tiny, but it's worth climbing over your suitcase a hundred times because the atmosphere in these spaces is magical. They are a gorgeous retreat from the cacophony of Marrakech's crowded, dusty streets.

Hôtel du Trésor is a traditional riad but the thing that makes it different is that the decor is rather eccentric and unusual. It's Fellini meets Marrakech – the decor consists of traditional Moroccan fixtures, then you'll come across European chandeliers in the bathroom or you'll have a Mona Lisa print on the wall. Some of the walls have been given the shiny tadelakt treatment. The reason there are so many little rooms in this house is because it used to be what's called a maison close or house of ill-repute. Indeed, I believe this area's still just a tiny little bit known for that. When this lovely old building's saviour, Adriano, found it, he fell instantly in love and saw nothing but potential. He first came to Marrakech on holiday ten years ago and really liked it. It was a time when Marrakech was becoming popular, people were starting to discover it, there was a lot of good energy and people were doing new things. The first bar was opened, the first disco, the first art gallery. The international community was small then and everyone knew each other and had parties.

Prior to moving to Marrakech, Adriano had had successful careers in fashion, cinema costume design and set decoration in Italy and Germany. He's very Italian looking with dark hair, dark eyes behind dark-rimmed glasses, olive skin and a Mediterranean temperament – erudite and funny one minute and yelling his head off the next. Anyone who's passionate about design or interior decor is always very inspired by Morocco. Adriano told me of the day he discovered the hotel: 'I heard the birds singing and I didn't understand where the singing was coming from, so I asked somebody in the street who said they have a tree in this courtyard. I came in and found out this was an old hotel from the fifties and I was very amazed because it was intact, with the charm of the fifties, and I really loved it. It is very unusual to find a riad which hasn't been redone in the seventies or eighties. The owner was an old man who was still making tea with the white blossoms from the orange tree. We developed a friendship, I would visit him to take tea and one day he said, "If you like it so much why don't you buy it?", so I did! There is a rumour that treasure is buried somewhere in this riad, which is why I called it Le Trésor.'

I have spent many hours in my favourite room 'La Giaconda' at Hôtel du Trésor, lying on the bed writing, eating dates, sipping red wine and listening to the birds singing in the orange tree. Adriano's very nice son Edis shares management duties with Amine, a tall, slim young man with aquiline nose and almond-shaped eyes. He is always polite and charming and has just produced his first child at whose birth he was present, which is unusual in Morocco. The other staff members are always lovely and if I ask for a glass of wine they don't just bring a glass of wine – they bring it on a deco tray with napkin, maybe some olives and always a quiet smile.

At the top of the riad is the little outdoor kitchen where the maids cook the breakfast breads, and where there are tables, chairs and parasols; and even further up another terrace with sun chairs and mirrored white wedding blankets on divans. Adriano likes putting items of decor together which are not really meant to be together and he is just the same with people. He loves introducing mismatched people to see what will happen. He believes this results in something new, amusing and creative. Adriano is very particular about details and sources a lot of his decor from the flea market at the Bab Khemis souk. It is very helpful for decorators like him that both foreigners and Moroccans never throw anything away – all is recycled, so it is easy to find things at Moroccan flea markets that you'd never see in Europe any more. When Jeff, Jane and I jumped in a petit taxi to film at the flea market, we found it absolutely stuffed with all the things Adriano loves – chandeliers, fifties and sixties furniture and lamp shades, old Moroccan doors, traditional tiles, old paintings and rugs, bevelled mirrors. The salon at Hôtel du Trésor is a sensational mix of art deco, black and white tiles, period armchairs and lovely French windows looking down to the courtyard. There is a public toilet on the first floor which is entirely mirrored from top to bottom with chrome lighting and fixtures. Nothing is ever too much trouble for Adriano – we needed another double room for our clients and he completely transformed the salon into a bedroom in an hour using bedroom furniture from his storage space. When we arranged for early evening cocktails, his perfectly trained and handsome staff did everything wonderfully – even putting up a big screen hung from the first floor to show my television show. From beginning to end, it has been a privilege to work with someone as professional, warm, witty and knowledgeable as Adriano.

The backbone of Morocco's hospitality industry is the women who cook and clean in the hotels, private homes and restaurants. You may have a flash French executive chef in a top restaurant, but if you look into the kitchen you will see women cooking, dressed in white with white bloomers or leggings underneath their smocks and white headscarves. They are the people who have the real knowledge because they have been cooking traditional food all their lives. They are not trained – they are born cooks. Adriano's cook Amina is one of these sterling young women. She still lives at home with her parents, dresses traditionally and has a high school education. She not only cooks for Adriano in his home, she cooks the breakfasts (her speciality is cakes) in the hotel and is available for private dinners. She speaks Italian to Adriano, French to me and Arabic to everyone else. Amina introduced me to the mellah market and all her contacts there – she runs the place with her big smile and sense of humour. She introduced me to the bread ovens, to the hammams where tangias are cooked, to the best place to buy roses and to unusual foods like the pastry which looks like fried string. In *Couscous and Other Good Food from Morocco*, Paula Wolfert talks about a pastry called azut cadi. You make the same dough as m'lawi and work it to a thin thread. While it is worked and being stretched, the completed portion is kept wrapped around a finger. When the thread is completed, it is left for twenty minutes and then it is flattened and fried in oil. After frying it is pressed down, which loosens the pastry and makes it look like a plate of spaghetti. It is best eaten fresh and warm, drizzled with wild honey.

Khubz (bread) is sacred in Morocco – sometimes you will see a piece of bread balancing on a door handle, usually because someone has respectfully picked it up off the street so as not to waste or soil it. In the medina most people don't have ovens so they make their bread at home and deliver it to the huge communal wood-fired oven nearest to them, then the kids pick it up on the way home from school at lunchtime. They make fresh bread again after lunch and send it to the oven with the kids going back to school, who then pick it up at the end of the day. They carry it on a pad on their heads. Sometimes the women just lean out of their doors and give the dough to the first person who passes and that person delivers it to the oven. The communal ovens also make bread for street stands, shops and restaurants. The first bread-making lesson I had in Morocco was at Dar Mima restaurant and I learned to make rolls. In the kitchen all was order, calm and extreme cleanliness – you could safely have had your appendix whipped out on the floor where the large pots, huge serving platters, baskets and tagines were stored. The cooks wrapped white scarves around their heads, then tied their long hair up in a knot with the tails of the scarf. It looked rather beautiful and graceful and much better than the nun method of tying scarves. The rest of the uniform was a white smock with a blue apron. I sat on a stool at the window between the kitchen and the dining room and watched girls blackening red capsicums on the huge shining professional stove, peeling (yes, peeling) cooked chickpeas, prepping huge bowls of carrots, turnips, pumpkin and courgettes, and rolling tiny meatballs from ground lamb and spices. Most of this prep happened at a low round table.

The chief cooks were two sisters, Saida and Tamou, of hugely disparate ages. They came from a family of ten and were taught to cook by their grandmother. When I rolled my eyes at the big family, they laughingly said nobody has big families like that now – two is enough. Saida, the younger one, had huge gold rings on her long brown fingers, the nails of which were painted with henna. She was very southern desert-looking with a long fine nose, full wide lips and almond eyes. She had African rather than Berber hair.

Very fine semolina, fresh yeast and salt was put in the gas'a with the right hand, then warm water was added with the left hand. For some reason they insisted the dough be mixed with the right hand. This dough is worked with the heels of the hands, not kneaded. Another technique they used, which is a Moroccan specialty, is pushing the dough with fists joined together, pressing downward, for about five minutes. The dough was then heeled into little balls and flattened out with the fingertips before being laid out to double in size on a clean white cloth. The rising time depended on the weather, but it usually took about an hour. Just before frying, the breads were sprinkled all over with coarse cornmeal, then cooked in oil for about three minutes on each side.

At Hôtel du Trésor Amina did more or less the same thing. Moroccan bread is porous and chewy with a soft crust – made for soaking up juices. Cooks usually use two parts of pale yellow semolina to one part of regular white flour. The best and very tasty bread, though, is made from coarser grains like barley and wholemeal with white flour. Nothing is measured – you just know. She puts the flour and semolina in the gas'a, mixes it with her hands, adds fresh yeast and salt then a bit of warm water. She keeps mixing until it is the right consistency then we both knead in the Moroccan style of pushing and folding for about five minutes. We break the dough into four pieces, roll it in semolina (sometimes they use cornmeal for this) then flatten it. We place it on a tray, cover with a tea towel and leave it to rise – they only raise dough once. We set off down the road into the sunken bread shop where men were shoving breads into the oven on long-handled paddles. The smell was fantastic, and when I asked them how they knew which bread belonged to which family, they replied, 'We know every wooden tray, Madame, and if we don't, they do.' Sometimes they mark the bread with a family seal or wooden stamp. I didn't see Amina making a secret mark, but in this magic land of honeyed dates and falling pomegranates, somehow, after a time of wonder, she knew which bread was hers.

Previous spread: *Making bread*
Above top: *Olive tree*
Above bottom: *Sorting olives*
Right and following: *Hôtel du Trésor*

Amina's Stuffed Bread

Amina made a stuffing from chopped onions, fresh coriander, salt, ground ginger, paprika and cumin. Having rolled out some dough in small flat discs she placed a heaped tablespoon of stuffing between two discs, pressed them together and baked them. Amina also cooks this stuffed bread on the barbecue or in a frying-pan.

We had a bread-making class with Radiga at Dar Tasmayoun and this was truly, deeply delicious because we cooked it in her wood-fired oven then ate it immediately. There is a big glamorous one outside the kitchen door, but she prefers to use the small oven behind her lodgings at the end of the garden. It's desperately cute and made from the same red clay everything else is made of – she and Fátima had built a wood fire and let it burn down, then they blocked the chimney with clay, placed the dough in and sealed the entrance with a big plate and wet sacks. In what seems like minutes, the bread is cooked and we are burning our fingers on it, stuffing bits into our mouths.

Kesra
Moroccan Bread

Makes 5 large flat breads

30 g fresh yeast or 1 tbsp dried
350 ml warm water
1 tsp sugar
200 g plain white flour
300 g semolina
1 tsp salt
2 tbsp extra virgin olive oil
1 egg yolk, beaten with a little water for the glaze
aniseeds

1. Put yeast, half the warm water and sugar in a small bowl to activate –
   takes about 10 minutes. It will start to bubble on the surface.
2. Sift flour, semolina and salt into a large bowl or onto the bench
   and make a well in the centre.
3. Into the well pour yeast mixture, half of the remaining warm water
   and the olive oil. Mix together to form a soft ball. Add more warm
   water if necessary. Turn out onto a floured bench and knead for
   10 minutes.
4. Divide dough into five pieces and knead into slightly flattened round
   balls. Flour a tray with semolina or fine cornmeal, put them on it,
   sprinkle with more semolina and cover with a clean cloth. Place in a
   warm corner of the kitchen and leave for 45 minutes to double in size.
5. Preheat oven to 200 °C (390 °F). Remove cloth, prick the rolls in three
   or four places, brush with egg yolk and sprinkle with a little cornmeal
   and aniseeds. Bake for 25 minutes until crisp and golden.

*When properly cooked, bread will sound hollow when you tap
it underneath. Moroccan cooks sometimes bake this bread in a
tagine dish.*

Another wonderful bread-type thing I tasted in the Fès medina was sfenzh or doughnuts, which in the souks of Morocco are feather clouds of deliciousness. They have to be eaten hot and dipped in sugar as you walk through the streets. The sfenzh cooker deftly plucks a little dough out of a pile and in the same movement makes a hole in the middle with his finger. This round is dropped in bubbling oil, puffs up and is scooped out to be threaded onto a shred of palm frond and knotted into a handle so you can carry it. The cook let me try, and of course I made little amoeba-shaped misfits with holes everywhere except in the middle.

Just before I dived into a makeshift café, I bought some green olives marinated in coriander and a slice of the white rounds of soft goat cheese you see everywhere in the medinas. I sat down and ordered mint tea, and another jolly man joined me, contributing his black olives and semolina bread. The cheese and doughnuts were delicious – it's so hard not to just eat all day in Morocco. No wonder the women are voluptuous. In the Arab world, fleshy is very desirable – it shows good health and wealth. For Moroccans, the ideal woman is very curvy, pale-skinned, not too cheeky and quite subservient by Western standards. Slim women are referred to as 'hska labsa saya' – a candle dressed in a skirt.

Sfenzh

Makes 12

1 tbsp yeast
1 tsp sugar or honey
250 ml (1 cup) warm water
500 g flour
½ tsp salt
1 litre vegetable oil
sugar for sprinkling

1. Mix yeast, sugar or honey and ¼ of a cup of the warm water and set aside to prove (takes about 10 minutes). It's ready when it starts bubbling.
2. Sift flour and salt into a mixing bowl, make a well in the centre and pour yeast mixture in. Mix in with your hand or a wooden spoon, adding enough warm water to make a firm dough.
3. Turn out onto a work surface, add a few more tablespoons of warm water and knead. Knead all the water in, from time to time picking the dough up and slapping it down. Add more water and keep kneading until all the water is incorporated and the dough is very spongy, elastic and quite wet. This takes about ten minutes.
4. Wipe mixing bowl then oil. Cover dough in oil and place it in the bowl. Cover with a tea towel and leave to rise in a warm place for an hour.
5. Heat oil in a deep fryer or pot to about 160 °C (320 °F). Have paper towels ready.
6. Put oil on your hands and squeeze out an egg-sized piece of dough between thumb and forefinger. Break it off with your other hand and make a hole in the middle by sliding your finger or thumb through. Swirl it around to enlarge the hole. When it resembles a doughnut, plop it into the hot oil.
7. Cook until dough puffs up and is golden – you may have to turn it over. Remove from the oil and drain on paper towels. Once you have done one to your satisfaction, you can do five at a time.

Serve hot, sprinkled with sugar. I have turmeric-flavoured cane sugar at home which goes very well with the sfenzh.

As we know, the rooftops are generally woman zones and at Hôtel du Trésor this is where the maids made the breakfast breads in the evenings, to be reheated the next morning. The privacy of the rooftop is essential for sanity in a place like Marrakech, where there is not one male who doesn't want something from you. The women, by contrast, are much softer, nicer and funnier. They are readily ribald and live in a world which is much more interesting, intimate and pleasant to be in. Their high voices sound like cooing doves to me. Every morning grateful people in hotels all over Marrakech arise from their pretty rooms and sit down to home-made jam, honey, tea, freshly squeezed orange juice and a pannier full of freshly baked, still-warm breads, which could be rghaif, beghrir (honeycomb pancake), croissant or some other treat. Nothing was ever too much trouble at Le Trésor and we loved the maids in pale smocks, head scarves and white bloomers.

All meals are served late in Morocco – they get up late. Lunch is early afternoon, le goûter is four or five o'clock and dinner can be at ten. I first had le goûter at Nadia's house in Larache. On a large, low, round table the servants brought in a cake made from cornmeal, yoghurt and olive oil (very moist and tasty), m'lawi with jam and honey, and little plates of spiced olives. Everything was eaten with the hands. Mint tea, coffee and fizzy drinks on a side table were served by Nadia, a lovely-looking, deliciously plump woman – someone with a sweeter, more dulcet nature you could never imagine. Her long black hair was slicked back into a bun, she was dressed traditionally but casually and I never saw her with shoes on.

I learned how to make m'lawi at another aunt's place. In the dim kitchen the maid was making what looked like bread rolls. I had to get my nose in. Like all Moroccan cooking, this addictive flat sort of puff pastry pancake was rather labour intensive. The process had many stages, but when you saw and tasted the final product it all made sense. This is what happened: first the maid mixed up the dough from white flour, a bit of starter from the dough of the day before, water and salt, then she divided it into small oblong rolls. As we walked in, she was covering a tobsil with melted butter. With her long black fingers she pressed the roll very long and flat in the tobsil, then folded it over lengthwise, all the while making sure she had lots of butter on her fingers. Next she rolled it up like a croissant, sprinkling the dough liberally with coarse cornmeal as she did so and rubbing more butter on – you can also use vegetable oil. These roll-ups were left to sit upright like tubes until she had finished making them all. Then she heated oil in a big, heavy-based black pan and flattened the roll-ups into pancakes – you could see the layers and folds of the making process. She fried them for about four minutes on each side. I thought they would be very greasy but they weren't at all because, after all, there was no oil in the base dough mixture. The result was a flaky, layered pastry inside with crunchy coat on the outside – divine when hot, drizzled with honey or sugar and eaten with mint tea. They invited us to stay for le goûter, but I had an invitation somewhere else. Seeing the desperate look on my face, the aunt grabbed a few hot m'lawi and wrapped them in a tea towel for me.

M'lawi

Makes 12

1 tbsp yeast
1 tsp sugar
6 tbsp warm water
450 g flour
½ tsp salt
300 ml warm water
peanut oil
½ cup coarse cornmeal
butter and sugar or honey for topping

1. Get yeast proving by combining yeast, sugar and the first measure of water. Allow to sit for ten minutes.
2. Sift flour and salt into a large, shallow wooden or earthenware bowl. Make a well in the centre into which you pour the yeast mixture and the second measure of warm water. Knead together until a smooth, elastic dough is formed. This is a wet, soft dough.
3. Divide into 12 balls and place on an oiled plate. Pour some peanut oil into a bowl. Place cornmeal in another bowl.
4. Oil a large, flat bowl or plate with your fingers.
5. Cover a dough ball with oil and flatten out into a long, thin oblong. Keeping fingers constantly covered in oil, sprinkle on a little cornmeal and fold dough over lengthwise. Spread more oil on and sprinkle a little cornmeal over. Roll up like a croissant and place standing up on oiled plate. Make the other m'lawi and leave to rise for half an hour.
6. Heat about half a centimetre of oil in a frying-pan. Flatten the pancakes with your fingers and cook for about two minutes on each side until golden and crisp.

Serve hot, topped with butter and honey or sugar and a glass of almond milk.

Worth mentioning is the divine **brik**, which is actually Tunisian but lots of Moroccans eat it, especially in the Rif Mountains. I was taught how to make them by Moroccan friends when I lived in Paris. The most traditional brik recipe is warka pastry filled with tuna and egg, folded over and fried. They can also be filled with kefta meatballs, matecha m'assala (tomato jam) or potatoes. Spring roll pastry is the closest consistency I have found to warka but you can also use filo. Like a soufflé, they have to be eaten immediately.

Brik

Serves 6

sunflower or other vegetable oil for frying
6 sheets warka or 6 x 21-cm square sheets of spring roll
   pastry or filo
200 g tinned or fresh chopped tuna
6 eggs
1 onion, minced
6 tbsp coriander, chopped
6 tbsp flat leaf parsley, chopped
sea salt
ground cumin
dried chilli flakes
1 egg white, beaten
lemon quarters for serving

1. Heat the oil in a shallow frying-pan.
2. Lay a pastry sheet on an oiled plate. Fold in two to mark it then open
   out. Put two tablespoons of tuna on one half and make a well in the
   centre. Into this, break an egg. Sprinkle on some onion, coriander and
   parsley and season with salt, a pinch of cumin and chilli to taste.
3. Brush pastry edges with egg white. Fold over into a triangle or half
   moon, depending on the shape of your pastry, and press the sides
   together. Repeat for each sheet of pastry.
4. Slide brik into the hot oil and fry for about a minute on each side until
   golden. Drain on paper towels and serve immediately. Squeeze lemon
   juice over.

*Serve with finger bowl provided with a slice of lemon and a rose
petal floating in it.*

Moroccans are in love with sugar and indulge their sweet tooth with fabulous sweet pastries. The souk has lots of pastry shops; their goods are loaded with enough sugar to kick-start an epidemic of Type 2 diabetes in the city. Quite often the vendors are just as syrupy – one guy in particular kisses foreign ladies' hands and declares undying love (or lust). They wouldn't talk to a Moroccan woman like that in a million years. But the best, most refined pâtisserie is in the Guéliz or new French town of Marrakech on Rue de la Liberté – the gastronomic tabernacle of Pâtisserie Al-Jawda, which most people call Pâtisserie Alami after the owner and pâtissière, Madame Alami. She was taught the recipes by her mother and now she and her sisters make them. The entire staff is women. For twenty-five years in this heavenly place there have been shelves and shelves of tiny, refined, blissfully worked pastries – the perfect sweet – one taste bud-stinging mouthful's worth. Enough to make you sigh, but not so much you would groan.

This is the realm of gems of artistic endeavour and beauty; rolled, triangled, snaked, stuffed, flowered, pocketed, crescented, powdered, sugared, almonded, dated, figged. There are maasems or Fátima's fingers, stuffed, rolled warka; kaab el ghazal, gazelles' horns stuffed with almond paste and dipped in orange blossom water; m'hanncha or serpents – a long pastry coiled, dusted with icing sugar and latticed with cinnamon powder; briouats made by wrapping warka around dates and figs in a triangle; shebbakia or deep-fried pastry ribbons, dunked in honey and sprinkled with toasted sesame seeds; ghreyba, a type of macaroon cake. There are huge dishes of the terrifically delicious amalou, a mixture of almond paste, honey and argan oil, which you spread on bread.

As we hopped around the shop, keeping out of the way of the compulsive floor washers, we were led to pondering the Moroccans' love of washing. They never give up on it. The entire time I was in that shop – and I mooned over every single pastry – the inundation of the floor never ceased. They bent over straight from the waist, keeping their backs perpendicular and slightly bending their knees – this is the Moroccan cleaning jack-knife position. Once when I was at the railway station on a busy mid-morning they locked all the travellers out to wash the floor – and I am not making that up. At our delicious hotel the decks seem to be sluiced approximately thirty-nine hundred times a day, but the place which takes the prize for sloshing endless buckets of water around is, of course, the hammam. One minute you're quietly sitting there meditating on the beauteous mountains of uninhibited flesh therein, and the next you're in a tidal wave gasping for air. If you had a psychopathology around hand-washing – for example, if you were Lady Macbeth – you would be in paradise in Morocco.

Kaab el Ghazal
Gazelle Horns

Makes approximately 40 pastries

For the almond paste:
250 g (1 cup) blanched almonds
125 g (½ cup) caster sugar
1 small egg
¼ tsp cinnamon
3 tbsp melted butter or vegetable oil
30 ml (2 tbsp) rosewater
½ tsp almond extract

1. Place almonds in food processor and process until powdered. Add other ingredients and blend to a sticky paste.
2. Roll heaped teaspoons of almond paste into little sausage shapes, fat in the middle and tapered at each end. Chill in fridge while making pastry.

For the pastry:
300 g (2¼ cups) white flour
½ tsp salt
3 tbsp melted butter or vegetable oil
90 ml (¹/₃ cup) orange water
90 ml (¹/₃ cup) cold water
oil in a little bowl for rolling the pastry
icing sugar for dusting

1. Place all ingredients aside from the icing sugar in the food processor and blend until a ball forms.
2. Knead by hand or with a dough hook in the mixer for 10 minutes. The pastry will be elastic and soft. Divide into four, rub in oil and leave on a plate.

This is an unusual pastry in that it has a lot of water and very little fat, so it requires a particular rolling method.

1. To make the gazelles' horns, sprinkle a little flour on the bench, take some oil from the bowl with your fingers and rub onto a rolling pin.
2. Roll out one of the quarters, pushing with the rolling pin to stretch the pastry. Sprinkle with a little flour if necessary, flip and keep rolling and stretching until pastry is thin like cardboard.
3. Preheat the oven to 200 °C (390 °F) and grease a baking sheet.
4. Press rounds out with an 8-cm diameter pastry cutter. Brush outer edges with water, place a sausage of almond paste towards the top half, fold pastry over and pinch edges together with fingertips.
5. Shape pastries into a horn or crescent with your fingers and place on baking sheet. Prick each horn with a fork to prevent expansion and splitting. Keep going until the rest of the pastry is used.
6. Bake for 10–15 minutes or until pale gold. Do not allow pastries to brown or they will harden.
7. Dust immediately with lots of icing sugar and serve piled up on an ornate tray.

Date and Apple Cigars

This delicious date and apple cigar recipe was kindly given to me by my Moroccan friend Simo of Simo's restaurant in Christchurch, New Zealand.

Makes 24 cigars

For the cigars:
100 g roasted almonds
100 g roasted pistachios
75 g caster sugar
2 tsp ground cinnamon
2 tbsp orange blossom water
1 egg yolk
150 g fresh dates, chopped
150 g apple, chopped
2 tbsp mint, chopped
12 sheets filo pastry
150 g clarified butter, melted
roasted sesame seeds
ground cinnamon

For the garnish:
100 ml liquid honey
sliced almonds
icing sugar
cinnamon

1. In a food processor combine nuts with sugar, cinnamon, orange blossom water and egg yolk to form a paste.
2. In a saucepan gently sauté dates and apple in a little butter for 5 minutes.
3. Remove from heat and add chopped mint and nut mixture. When cool, divide into six.
4. Cover filo pastry sheets with a slightly damp tea towel. On a dry surface lay one sheet of filo, brush with butter, some sesame seeds and a little cinnamon. Lay another sheet on top of the first and do the same thing.
5. Take one of the six lots of the stuffing and form into a long finger. Lay it along the short edge of the filo and roll it up to look like a long cigar.
6. Do this five more times, then cut each roll into four. Preheat the oven to 150 °C (300 °F).
7. Lay cigars in a shallow roasting pan and brush with butter. Bake for 15 minutess or until golden and crisp.
8. Remove from oven and pour honey over. Sprinkle sliced almonds on top.
9. When cool, sprinkle with icing sugar and cinnamon.

What you have with pastries is coffee. Coffee in Morocco is not exactly sensational. In the cafés, which are almost entirely frequented by men, coffee is made French espresso and also Turkish style. At Latifa's place they made coffee at home by serving me glasses of hot milk into which I could stir as much Nescafé as I wanted! Another more palatable method is called café cassé – a glass of strong black coffee 'broken' with a little milk. At Café des Épices in the medina, they serve what they call nus-nus (half and half), which is half milk and half espresso coffee – it's very good. Another unusual way of drinking coffee in Morocco is to add ras el-hanout to the brew. Say you were making plunger coffee for four people, you would put four heaped tablespoons of ground coffee into the jug along with quarter of a teaspoon of ras el-hanout, then pour the boiling water in.

In keeping with their love of anything sweet, Moroccans are, of course, mad about honey – especially wild honey. Morocco is literally a land of milk and honey, the twin symbols of prosperity and abundance. Specialist shops sell a variety of honey, royal jelly and pollen, all of which keep you young and beautiful for ever. The honey is of very good quality and used a lot in cooking by all strata of society; but genuine, pure honey is hard to come by and people have a tendency to buy cheaper Spanish stuff of doubtful purity. The prices can range from 40 dirham a kilo to the best Pur Zakkoum at 140 dirham. Most is produced traditionally by families, some taken from the wild and some farmed. Thyme honey is almost black, zakkoum is dark red, orange honey is yellow, and some mountain honeys from the south are as clear as water – the hives being found in mountain fissures and high up in tree trunks. Vast eucalyptus forests, plantations of citrus, fields of sunflowers, and mountains covered in rosemary, lavender, thyme and wild flowers are all fodder for the busy bees in the Gharb region of southern Morocco. Jbal is a honey made from bees who only eat figs. Specialties like all the goûter and breakfast breads and crêpes, briouates, all the little pastries, pastillas, sauces reduced with prunes and honey, would be unthinkable without this product. And we all know how good it is for us as an antibiotic, tranquilliser, antiseptic and anti-rheumatic; and when all else fails, as was proven in *The Perfumed Garden*, honey is an aphrodisiac and improves sexual performance. I bought a big jar of the best, because you never know when you're going to be called upon for a strong sexual performance.

Sometimes you get invited to the home of an expat who loves English-style food. My friend Jonathan met me and my friend at the door to his apartment one melting evening.

'Ah,' he said, 'there you are. I sent Mr Lhascen to bring you here in a taxi. No doubt he spent the money on cigarettes and made you walk. Am I correct?'

'Yes,' we beamed, but we don't mind. We had such interesting conversations with him and we think him angelic.'

'How lovely for you, but I feel bound by conscience to tell you he is deaf. Mr Lhascen has been with me for years, I call him my homme à tout faire, when he is in fact my man who does nothing. There is not one thing this man does correctly yet I'm very, very fond of him. When I was ill he never left my side, carrying me to and from the bathroom and dressing me.'

Mr Lhascen smiled broadly and nodded. Jonathan led us past the kitchen where we were introduced to the cook, Mr Tizini, and out onto a terrace, overflowing with honeysuckle, singing birds and plants. We sat in a shady sort of pergola and shook hands with a dark, handsome Moroccan called Abdelsalem, who was introduced as 'the fixer'. Tall, slightly portly and expansive, Jonathan was dressed in linen shirt, beige jacket with hankie in the pocket, dark pink jeans, shoes and socks, his hair was combed straight back and his blue eyes sparkled in what seemed like a permanently amused face. It was 35 °C, I was pouring with sweat, yet the Moroccan staff remained as cool as cucumbers, with their protective brown skin and slow movements.

'Mr Lhascen,' Jonathan bellowed, 'get some gin and tonics for Madame Peta and her friend and don't give them ice – they can't drink Moroccan water or they will be sick.'

Mr Lhascen put up his hands in horror and said, 'Jonathan, you don't have to say these loud words. I hear you, but I not going to move because I in love with Madame Peta's friend. I look her. I not move.'

'Oh, for God's sake, Mr Lhascen, go and get the gin.'

A huge pet cock roamed freely in the flat – a cock which didn't know what it was. It fell in love with furniture and tried to mate with it; and exhibited its misogynist pathology by attacking women's feet. The last female guest got three painful bites on her leg and foot, they got infected and she had to be hospitalised. It was particularly attracted to painted toenails and I was obliged to keep my feet up or hide behind furniture.

'Peta, please don't write that I am just a poof with a big cock – my mother doesn't need this information. Michael Palin was in Tangier filming recently, did a segment on me here in the flat and the cock became a major part of the story. The crew loved my bird but you don't seem to have the same affection.'

Presently we were called inside to the dining room for lunch, which was overcooked carrots and beans, potato cakes and salad. For our benefit Mr Tizini had been dressed up in serving clothes with a Fès hat. Jonathan loved the lunch and remarked that it had taken him ages to teach Mr Tizini how to cook proper English-style food. The flat was resplendently English in decor, with plush couches, red walls, very good paintings, desks with books on them and heavy curtains. As soon as it was polite to do so, we snuck into the kitchen and there we found Mr Lhascen and Mr Tizini eating their lunch with their fingers – a golden tagine with whole fish, tomatoes and waxy yellow Moroccan potatoes. I gasped in envy and they immediately jumped off their chairs and insisted we sit down and share it with them.

On another visit we bought huge bunches of flowers for Jonathan and his household. The seller had made up little bunches for us. He filled the bouquet wrappings with rose petals and nearly jumped out of his skin with rapture when we kissed him. Upon arrival at Jonathan's for cocktails, we sprinkled the petals all along his hallway and gave satellite bouquets to the servants, who accepted them with shining eyes. The salon was garnished with English expats; the rooster looking longingly at my feet with their alarm lights of red nail polish. One woman was got up in an extraordinary outfit, considering the heat, of Afghani skirt with mirrors, white cotton blouse, white stockings and red pumps. Her husband was dressed in suit and tie. Another wealthy Englishwoman was there with her 'what ho' ex-husband, who was dressed entirely in white right down to his shoes. Her present husband, a younger Moroccan, was not there but I was told he was a sensational gardener. When I asked to see her extensive gardens she declined, saying they weren't at their best and I was to come back earlier in the summer next year. I felt disinclined to explain that I lived on an island in the South Pacific and might not want such a long walk. Mr Tizini darted around with slices of pizza from down the road. He was dressed in his entertaining finery and served the slices on a Georgian silver platter. I loved Jonathan and felt completely comfortable with his eccentricity – his expat life is all part of the colourful fabric of Morocco.

An important and fun thing to do when in
Morocco is to go shopping. They are very
good at suede sofa throws, contemporary
kilims (rugs), wall lanterns in Florentine
porcelain, jewellery, leather belts, wrought
iron candlesticks and embroidered household
linen. But they're not so great at clothes
unless you know where to go. Souk shopping
is hilarious and haggling is a part of it.
Moroccans, especially those from Marrakech,
will good naturedly follow you down the
street to continue the haggling game. Europeans are disinclined
to do this but you have to relax and see it as enjoyable rather than
embarrassing. Also there is absolutely no need to lose your temper or
be rude – Moroccans don't understand that. They adore haggling and
consider you a fool if you just accept the first price – they would never
accept the first price for anything.

The souk is not just for tourists; it is like the local mall for the
medina inhabitants. Unfortunately, Moroccan women specialise in
displaying a very ugly taste in clothes. I would like to go there and
completely redesign all their gear. Not just the shape but also the
colours. They choose really dull, muddy colours and fabric that is not
natural. The shape of the jellaba (a flowing robe with a hood) and the
kaftan is straight up and down because you're hiding your sexuality –
you're hiding your shape – and a lot of women use the hoods so they
can also hide their heads. They don't wear these robes at home – it's
a garment you put on for modesty to go out and then as soon as you
get home you take it off and get your high heels out! Morocco is the

most modern of the North African countries, so in the street men dress in jellaba or Western clothes, and the women in anything from chic Western, to westernised-modest-Arab (ill-fitting pant suits), to jellaba over leggings, to fully covered with hood and veil. I saw some women in extraordinary black outfits with only half slits for their eyes. With gloves, socks, head scarf, which came right down to the eyes and face veil right up to almost meet it – not one skerrick of flesh was exposed. How these women managed to drive or cross the road without peripheral vision is a mystery. You could be dead before you saw a donkey coming. When I asked about them people replied with disdain, 'They are not Moroccan, they are Kuwaiti.'

The jellaba is the greatest de-sexualiser ever invented. No woman, no matter how beautiful, could look good in this garment – unless you put a belt on it, which they usually do if it's a party. The shapelessness of it makes you look like a bag of overcooked couscous, and the scarf is unflattering – the way it is folded on the sides of the face then pinned under the chin so no wicked hair can be glimpsed to drive men to distraction. In India the women are also expected to dress modestly but they have found a very beautiful way of doing it with gorgeously coloured saris and flatteringly cut salwar kameez – tunic, pants and scarf over-the-shoulder outfits. I must say, though, that after a month in Morocco I started to think there were some benefits to a jellaba: (a) they protect you from the filth of the medina; and (b) the constant hassling by men ceases when there is nothing to see. After much enquiry, I came to the conclusion that the way a woman dresses in Morocco is entirely a matter of choice; it comes down to how she or her controller (father, brother or husband) interprets Islam. Nowhere in the Koran does it say women have to be covered up.

In Essaouira I saw quite a lot of women wrapped in cream blankets called haiks, some with black face veils and some with cream. The fabric came down low to their brows and the veil rose right up to their soporific eyes. This is not a shapeless garment like the jellaba, but infinitely beautiful and secretive, full of shadows and folds. It appeared to be one large piece of fine, soft, creamy wool wrapped and folded in a mysterious way. All you could see were the hands and the ankles and feet. I found out later that these are the Regraga women, part of an uncommon and secretive Berber tribe. It is said they have a collective memory full of secrets, and they are called the tmarsit of the countryside. Wandering in and out of wild figs on the branches of a sterile fig tree are insects that pollinate. Without these insects, the tmarsit, the figs would fall off unripe and unfertilised.

'Wherever the Regraga pass there is fertility; where they don't pass there is sterility.' They are wanderers doing a constant circular pilgrimage, or sort of stroll, which links the milestones of their horizons, symbolically unifying this endless route. The eastern Regrada clans symbolise the sun and earth, and the western clans the moon and sea. I was desperate to ask these mysterious women how they folded their haiks but didn't dare approach them. When I asked a young woman in Western clothes about them she said the haiks were worn before the jellaba came in.

I'm not saying all of these Moroccan garments are dull and unattractive to me; in fact many Moroccan designers create exquisite kaftans and the wedding kaftans are sensational. I went to a wedding in Kenitra and there was no question that I turn up dressed in Western clothes, so the wardrobes were ransacked for a suitable, formal jellaba. I was given a spectacular outfit or takchita composed of the outer robe embossed with gold braid, diamantes and beads, and an under kaftan to line it. Basically it meant wearing two heavy dresses in the heat, drawn in at the waist by a wide, ornate, gold-embroidered belt. The bride herself would wear something like this and also be laden down with so much gold jewellery and head decoration that she resembles a halcyon goddess. I love all the over-the-top glamour of a good kaftan, but I craved something lighter and more modern.

On my wanderings in my area of the souk I came across a tiny shop on Riad Zitoun selling sexy kaftans. It is called Kasbek and is owned by a couple of Australian expats – Cassandra Karinsky and Rebecca Wilford. They have featured on the pages of Spanish and Australian Vogue magazines and specialise in vintage kaftans, redesigned for fashion-conscious women who admit they have a shape. The girls go on trips into the villages to buy second-hand, vintage kaftans that may have only been worn twice. They clean and reshape them to fit tightly so they still cover you but are flattering. Mostly they are long to the floor, clasped under the bust, open from there down and worn with jeans or black pants underneath. Moroccan women wear kaftans that are long enough so that when they have the belt cinched and are in high heels, the dress just touches the ground. There is just the small issue that both Cassie and Rebecca are very pretty and shapely so if you see them in their kaftans you enjoy the illusion that you are going to look just like that. I had spied lots of second-hand and vintage kaftans in the spice souk of Rahba Kedima Square, so decided to take my gastronomads there for a kaftan hunt. Well, you can perhaps imagine the hard sell when a group of Europeans start trying things on in the middle of the souk. Kaftans were flying everywhere and we were all fancying ourselves as Cassie of Kasbek, spotting 'potential' left and right. I was fortunate enough to get the pick of the souk – a fabulous pink and green silk flowery vintage kaftan with handmade gold braid all around it. A few days later I looked just like Cassie – minus the blonde bombshell looks.

What you need to go with a good kaftan is a good handbag. For some God-unknown reason, when I was in Fès I asked to see the **tannery** pit. The tannery was deeply and grossly horrific both in sight and smell – like a medieval leper colony. It was unbelievable to think we were breathing and standing in the twenty-first century but actually experiencing the fifteenth! The rank odour of rotting flesh forced tourists to put bunches of mint up to their noses. Moroccan leather is the finest in the world and always has been – witness the French word for leather worker: maroquinier. The strictly male tannery, like an open fetid quarry, had skins in various states of 'freshness' all over the place – some still had blood on, some had been scraped and others were drying. Donkeys, the poor things, brought them in and hurriedly trotted out again. Cheerful-looking men sat on stones with hides on their laps, scraping the guck and hair off. They wore protective pants but the stuff got all over them. They must belong to some macabre guild with terrifyingly antiquated health and safety regulations. They also used fantastic ingredients to help them in their work, such as cow urine, fish oils, pigeon excrement, animal brains and fats, sulphuric acid and chromium salts.

The next location on the trip was the dyer's souk, which also smelled like an open graveyard. It was full of dyeing vats made from mud brick and tile. The dyes are all natural – saffron for yellow, poppies for red, indigo for blue and antimony (black sulphide) for black. Men in bare feet stirred the hides with long sticks, piling them up on the sides then laying them out on the straw to dry. The rinsing was done in the street so that the pavement took on different colours depending on the time of day.

I spoke earlier of Moroccan **weddings** – let me tell you about my experience. It takes five days to get married in Morocco: the first day is the henna day, the second the trousseau day, the third the hammam day, the fourth the present day and the fifth the wedding day. The family connection for this wedding was on my friend Hicham's side – his nephew was the groom. I arrived on 'Le Jour du Henné' – the henna day. In another house on the other side of town the bride's family was having a separate henna party with her family. As I knew Hicham was one of eighteen children and he often mentioned his two mothers, I suspected it would be quite a big do. We piled out of the car at a large two-storeyed house in a swish suburb, took our shoes off at the door, and entered a sumptuous salon, the walls of which were lined with at least thirty women, all close family members, all dressed in sparkling finery, most wearing scarves. I was introduced to each and every one, and all of Hicham's sisters were pointed out to me. Hicham's second mother (his other mother is deceased) was a beautiful, slight old lady with bright hennaed hair under her white scarf and a tattoo on her chin – one line going down, with three dots on either side. When I asked about the tattoos I was told they are not done very often now, except in isolated villages, and are for decoration if jewellery is scarce. Women used to tattoo between their eyebrows, and on their neck, feet, wrists and breasts.

Everyone was talking animatedly and drinking fizzy drinks and mint tea. Every single person had to know who I was and why I was writing everything down. A group of wedding musicians arrived, dressed up in finery, with all sorts of exotic instruments. Placing themselves firmly in the middle of the room, they struck up a tune and the place went mad. This family loves to dance and it was obvious who the visitors from outside were – they were far more circumspect. Adila, Hicham's sister, and all the other sisters hit the dance floor stamping, belly dancing, screaming and you-youing with children and teenagers of both sexes. Nowhere was a man to be seen, so when we took a break from dancing, I asked Adila where they were.

'Upstairs in a separate room,' she said. 'It is tradition to keep apart and in the old days the entire three days or week of a wedding was conducted separately. Men never saw women dancing – women only danced for themselves.'

'So what do the men do in their room?'

'They smoke and talk – serious men's talk.'

'They don't have music and dance and get loose?'

'No. But on the last big wedding day everyone is together and everyone dances.'

'With eighteen children and their children to marry off, there must have been a lot of parties in this house. Do you go to all this trouble for each one?'

'Yes, of course. For each and every one. We love it.'

Adila adored a party. She was always the first to dance and sing, and was right in the thick of everything organising, bringing drinks and, later, the food. She had tucked up a corner of her jellaba into her belt so you could see her beautiful brown legs. While all this action went on the young, good-looking bridegroom sat passively in state in the centre against the wall, wearing a white jellaba and red Fès hat. He was surrounded by flowers and little girl cousins who were beside themselves with all the excitement. I could smell food, so walked through the house until I found it. There in the garage were dadas, the professional wedding caterers, squatting on little stools over huge pots of stews. It worked like this: first the men upstairs got fed, then the women downstairs, then the servants and helpers. Low round tables were brought in, and bowls and jugs for hand-washing passed around. Giant chicken tagines and baskets of bread were placed in the centre of each table and we dived in with our hands. Satiated, I lay back on the banquette while the table was cleared for the next course – a couscous piled up with beef, prunes, green olives and preserved lemons.

I groaned. The feast was finished off with fruit platters with the knives sticking out of them and hand-washing. After dinner I went out the back of the house and found all the helpers and servants eating the best bits of the feast/beast – heads, offal, feet and so on. They were in heaven in their bare feet with juices dribbling down their chins.

The food at a wedding is very symbolic, and is placed under divine protection. A week before the wedding the mother will offer the bride dishes that 'no ladle has stirred' so her marriage will be peaceful and untroubled. For prosperity the mother-in-law gives the bride a loaf of bread as soon as she arrives in her house. Before and after the wedding the bride visits the hammam to purify herself. When she gets home her parents bring her mint tea or coffee flavoured with orange flower water and cinnamon, and such delicacies as soft boiled eggs, roasted almonds and krachels – little sweet brioche with aniseed and sesame seeds. As I was to find out, the rituals at the henna day are a mixture of Mediterranean folklore, paganism, Islam and modern Western ideas. And nobody seemed to know why things are the way they are.

It was now late at night, but no one showed signs of flagging. The musicians had come back, blowing two immensely long trumpets very loudly to announce the commencement of the henna ceremony. Everyone gathered around the groom, his mother sitting on his left, singing and clapping. Someone lit candles on a little table in front of him and his palms were painted with henna. Then one of the sisters pulled the hood over his head and face, and proceeded to wind a length of fabric around it like a turban. This was accompanied by much trilling and drumming, and the fabric was unwound and the process repeated three times. The boy sat quietly and allowed himself to be swathed and unswathed. When I asked Adila why all these things were done, she said with her beautiful, almond-eyed smile, 'Parce que.'

I said, 'Parce que quoi?'

She said, 'Parce que c'est comme ça. C'était toujours comme ça.'

The hood was then lifted and everybody kissed him and sprinkled orange water over him, also branches of mint and marjoram to symbolise sweetness, purity, prosperity and happiness. Amid all the noise and laughing and carrying on, people started throwing money onto the little table. Then it seemed to be over, the groom was allowed to leave the room and Zohra announced she was tired and wanted to go home.

On the way we passed another wedding in full throes of the final day, so I jumped out of the car to have a look. What I saw was hundreds of people dancing and eating fabulous food like pastilla, and in the distance the bride and groom being carried around in a big shell. I'm not kidding. The waiting staff were decked out in fanciful costumes. The bride and groom seemed to submit to rather than enjoy all the carrying around in thrones, kiosks, gazebos, bronze buckets and various extravagant receptacles. The beautiful bride had diamantes stuck on the outer corners of her eyes and appeared to be in a trance. They went backwards and forwards all over the place, were fussed with and endured five outfit changes that were ever more extravagant. Paradoxically, the final earth-shattering one, the pinnacle of the wedding, the one that shows the parents really are bankrupting themselves, is a white, European-style wedding dress. I found this most incongruous. Meanwhile, the exhausted couple, who had by this stage been partying, dressing up, dressing down and ritualising day and night for at least four days, showed no emotion. They behaved like the Queen on Valium, and really, when you come to think of it, these people are royalty for a day and it is probably the only time in their lives it will happen. But even this is not the end, because a few days after the wedding the newlyweds must cook the achat el-hout, a fish dinner, for their family and friends.

'This carry-on must cost a fortune,' I muttered to Mohamed.

'It does,' he replied, 'and it's a huge waste of money. People spend their whole lives paying off their children's weddings. You could buy a house for the cost of a wedding.'

Chapter Five
Safi & Sardines

I had visited the magical, chilled-out, coastal town of Essaouira on previous forays to Morocco and at one point David and I considered basing our gastronomic adventure there. Driving into Essaouira offers a wonderful sight – magnificent curved beach, blue water, huge fishing boats, windsurfers and mysterious mistiness. This town was called Mogador (probably a phonetic adulteration of Sidi Mogdoul, a local saint) when the Portuguese controlled it in the fifteenth century, and the old pink fortifications and city wall are testimony to that ancient past. They lost it in the sixteenth century, whence it fell to rack and ruin. In the eighteenth century the King decided to make Mogador the most important port town in Morocco. After all, it had a temperate climate, opened onto the world and had a multiethnic, famously hospitable population. In fact, for a long time Essaouira was the only Moroccan port open to outside commerce. The guardians of Islam were against opening up trade to Europe for fear of the pious Islamic soul being perverted by outside contact with sinful infidels. This fear was overridden by the forward-thinking King who hired the famous French architect Theodore Cornut to design a harmonious town that would be perfect for trade. It was renamed Essaouira, meaning 'well designed'. When the French turned up in 1912 they called it Mogador again, and when they were thrown out the Moroccans renamed it Essaouira. Essaouira/Mogador is unique in the whole of Morocco, heavy with a glorious silence and calm, a complete paradox in light of its appearance of vivacious worldliness. It is a place which, for century after century, has been told it is beautiful and seems to react in serenity and happiness, as if it were only natural. The decline it fell into under the French is being shrugged off and this loved, much-poeticised town is getting its self-confidence back.

Upon arrival at Essaouira, a little man with a cardboard peak tied to his head with string transported my bags in a cart to my hotel. I trotted along behind him, through the huge rampart doors into the old town – everything was pale and bleached in the permanent sunny haze. The carrier tried to charge me 30 dirham for a 10 dirham transport job, which I smartly put paid to. I dumped the bags and wandered out to survey my territory. I was suddenly washed with a feeling of happiness at having decided to come here. Essaouira had a very good feeling, and between the hotel and the restaurant I had been recommended, only three men hissed at me, albeit perfunctorily. How winsome that they call to 100 gazelles in a day and never get disheartened at being ignored. This, I decided, could turn out to be heaven where even a foreign woman with red hair and freckles could get a break. A girl sitting next to me on the bus had advised me to eat at El-Ayoune in the picturesque area under the big clock.

The best part about walking under the big clock was the tiny hole-in-the-wall CD shop, which blared gnaoua (pronounced nawa) music and the powerful, colourful, controlled voice of Oum Kalsoum all day. The young man who ran the shop was a very tall, dark Saharan Moroccan wearing an electric blue shirt and a 100-watt smile. I got into musical raves with him almost every time I passed by. I found out lots from him about Oum. At my hotel the Sahara boys played their jazzy, cymbally, double bassy, repetitive gnaoua. I can see why Jimi Hendrix and Mick Jagger liked Essaouira and the infectious music – the place is mesmerising and naturally lends itself to free jazz mixings. Gnaoua is technically a spiritual brotherhood of descendants from slaves brought to Morocco from Central and West Africa. As a music it is used to help dancers go into a trance and invoke spirits. Hashish helps quite a lot, too.

In the coastal cities you also hear al-Andalusian music played with an oud (lute) and a soft drum. The women clap their hands to the music and dance in a sort of Egyptian/Spanish mélange of belly dancing and flamenco. The lute has a distinctly soft, exotic sound and is played with one single and five double strings. The long neck faces backward half way up, and there don't appear to be frets. The drum is not just an accompaniment – there seems to be a question and answer sequence going on. The singing sounds medieval, and there is no body language to speak of, but the result is very beautiful and unusual. The words lament the loss of the Alhambra, of Spain grieving for Andalusia and hoping paradise will prove sympathetic. Classic al-Andalusian music is an ancient and rich relic of the Muslim Andalusians, now only surviving in Morocco. It came over when Granada fell in 1492, resting in the palaces of Rabat, Oujda and Tétouan, that most Hispano-Mauresque of all Moroccan towns.

In that blessed era, under the sun of Seville, Córdoba and Granada, a golden age of civilisation flourished. In 822 BC a brilliant musician called Zirab left a decadent oriental court for Andalusia, where he discovered fertile ground for his music. Moroccans call this music 'al-ala', meaning it is instrumental rather than sung. Zirab developed a system of twenty-four suites known as the nawba, which play on the alternate use of rhythm and non rhythm. With the passage of time only eleven suites have survived, listed and written down in the seventeenth century by a nostalgic music lover in Tétouan called Al Hayk. The nawbas are tightly structured and correspond to the same number of harmonic modes of Andalusian music. This is a brilliant system, as each is supposedly in tune with an hour of the day. The greatest contemporary exponent of this music is the now deceased Mohamed Larbi Temsamani. He was not only a distinguished lutenist and violinist but also adapted the piano to the nawba.

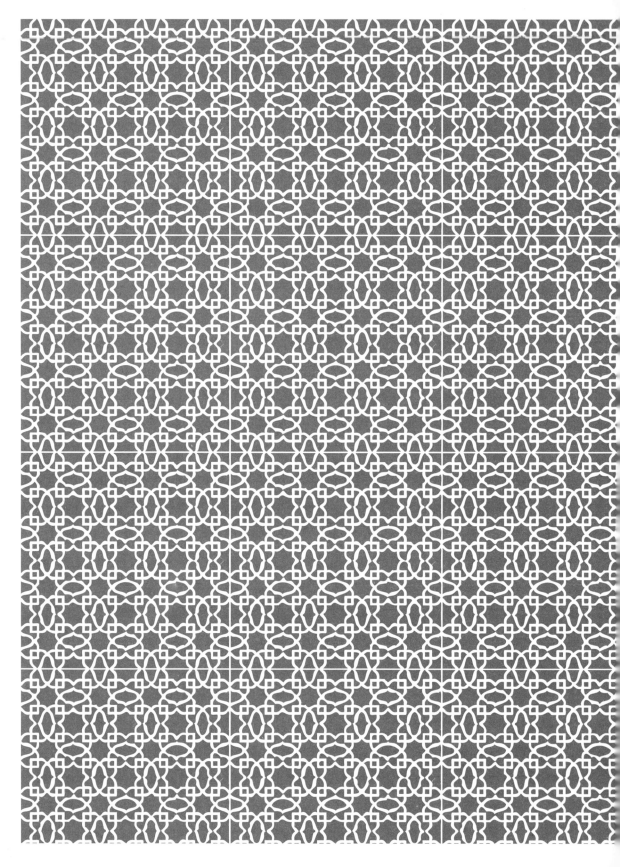

Fish is what you eat in Essaouira; they're inundated with fish and everyone who has been there says, 'You must eat the grilled fish on the beach at sunset', so I did. What these visitors omit to explain is how you eat fish on the beach in a 50-kilometre-an-hour wind. When I arrived the wind was down and it was sunny, so I was lulled into a false sense of security. From the chalkboard list of freshly caught possibilities, I chose a whole daurade (sea bream), which was split open, emptied and locked up in a folding grill. While it was cooking on the fire, I ate with my fingers a portion of that ubiquitous salad of chopped tomatoes, onions and capsicums with oil and lime juice. I couldn't see a thing because of the darkness, which falls suddenly in Essaouira, but I think with that and the wind I ate a whole lot of hair, sand and delectably tender fish. No serviettes unless you asked and hands washed under a nearby hose. I went back to that beach the next day to sunbathe. Within half an hour my body was completely covered in fine layers of limpid sand, which could not be brushed off. It was in my hair, up my nostrils, in my nails and somehow stuck to my skin – no matter how much I washed. It stayed with me for days.

Wandering down to the port where, incidentally, Orson Welles shot the opening of his film *Othello*, I found myself in the fish market, which was empty owing to the high wind. Two men were singing a song in French and asked me if I knew the title and singer. They thought it was 'La Femme Dans Mon Lit' and I thought it was sung by Aznavour but they weren't so sure. I moved on to the heart of Essaouira, the port full of little stands selling just about everything you could lay a name to – seashells, mint tea, pastries, stingrays, sardines, crabs, sea bream, pageot, tassergal (a sort of blue fish like tuna), turbot, mackerel, swordfish, shrimps, lobster, clams, palaya, sole. Further along the quay in the belly of the port were the huge, beautifully crafted fishing boats. One of the favourite pastimes of people in Essaouira is to sit at one of the rooftop cafés or restaurants at sunset with a chilled rosé and watch the fishing boats coming in. Officially there are 2400 fishermen, 39 fixed units and 300 fishing boats, the trawlers being much more profitable than the sardine boats. Strangely enough, despite their popularity, there are few sardines in Essaouira waters, most of the supplement coming from neighbouring Safi.

The unique thing about this port is the constant construction and repairing of boats, some legal, some not. Well, the boats are actually built in workshops near the port and finished off at the port, but you have to be officially registered. Fishermen regularly ignore this rule and police regularly confiscate their boats. Not only does it take at least a year for a new boat to get authorisation to sail, but the Souiri (those from Essaouira) themselves are old-fashioned in their ways and the boats are badly equipped. They are unwilling to install depth sounders, essential for knowing the depth of the water and other basic equipment – their most sophisticated equipment is a radio – so they work much harder and longer than they have to, just to get a catch. It's not unusual for fishermen to spend thirty-six hours at sea. On top of being old-fashioned, some of them are stubborn and refuse to cast their nets anywhere but where they have always cast them. They are also superstitious and won't make boats of steel because they are afraid of anything iron, which for them symbolises death. And it is rumoured that Spanish fishing boats pilfer the best from Moroccan waters anyway. What do the Souiri fishermen say? 'The fisherman is like the farmer; he throws his line and he waits. It is God who decides the rest.'

At the same time, I sympathise with the traditional fisherman.

This way of fishing in pretty blue, white and green wooden boats is long-established, and these people have a system of haulage for repair which is unique in the world, designed to respect the fragility of traditional boats and not damage them. This patrimony must be protected as the last stand of a naval tradition which threatens to disappear in the flick of a fish tail. The fishermen were pulling up fish from the hold in woven baskets and transferring them from hand to hand up to bright yellow containers. All around the boats people were buying fish, and along the quay buildings very poor women squatted in front of their meagre piles of sardines, gutting them on the spot. I turned down amorous offers from smelly, fishy men in jaunty hats scrunched and twisted to resemble a tagine lid, my good nose leading me to a seaside bar (yes bar!) next to the Chalet de la Plage restaurant. Tiny bar full of men – too bad. I was desperate for a beer and sat down and ordered. Possibly the best beer I've ever had was followed in quick succession by another two. I sat there for an hour enjoying an unhindered view of the last fishing boats coming in surrounded by fluttering seagulls in the thick air.

By now it was late afternoon and the souk was opening up again, not too crowded, the people strangely enigmatic and sweet and gentle, like Safi and so different from the rest of Morocco. The Souiris are more a traditional community than a society with classes, politics and organisations, and not taken to spontaneity or frivolity. They are calm and relaxed, by and large. It was in the middle of the fabulous souk, overflowing with produce and shops, that the universe provided me with a raffia shoe shop, which was to lead to that month's sartorial downfall. Deciding to have a pair specially made for me because the choice of approximately 3000 was insufficient, I proceeded to share the experience with passers-by, other customers, the shoemaker's family and the man who delivered the mint tea. They encouraged me to try on every shoe in the shop three times, terminating with the idea of a green, beige and red pair. The monetary deal being struck, you then sit down on a little stool to mainline sugar cleverly disguised as mint tea. But the universe wasn't finished with me, because no sooner had I left this shop than I walked one pace and there was another, even grander shoe shop with wildly exotic designs involving beads, pompoms, lime green, lime yellow, dusky pink and burnt orange. I entered and repeated exactly the same procedure. An hour later I emerged with a pair of pink leather and yellow raffia Aladdin-style babouches with a long, bendable tassel on the toe, which could be manipulated into any shape you fancied. I also had some neutral coloured raffia platforms and some pink and beige mules which clackety-clacked wonderfully on the footpath.

Back into the throng of the now much busier and darkening souk, I witnessed the life and death cycle of a chicken in the space of a block – a repeated sight in Morocco. I also found stalls with eight varieties of plump, juicy dates and every kind of dried fruit imaginable – figs, apricots, raisins, prunes. It's wonderful being in the souk at night under the navy-blue sky, winding up and down the narrow alleys with your basket, getting lost and then suddenly finding yourself in front of your hotel without having the slightest idea how you did it.

A short wander the next morning brought me to the large, perfectly designed central square, Place Prince Moulay Hassan, where a girl could get the three things she needs in life – a French newspaper, a coffee and an internet café. Once these three are done with, the rest of the day can only go heavenward. Of all the bustling, hip cafés on the square I chose Café Ben Mostapha because it seemed to have 1900 flies instead of the 2000 in the other places – must be the fish. Here I often spent hours drinking coffee and orange juice, reading the paper, talking to other visitors and watching the rather chic world go by. Maybe a Frenchman in a wide-brimmed straw hat, pressed white linen jacket and Italian shoes; maybe a gaggle of blanketed Regraga women with black eyes; maybe the boys selling croissants and pain au chocolat; maybe street performers; maybe families doing the passa promenade if it was Sunday; maybe a policeman in tandem with a soldier. All in the thick mist and pleasantly warm temperature, with the sun there, but not intruding. A striking thing in Morocco is the number of decrepit and very old, falling-apart-looking people resembling black puppets in black rags with deeply lined faces like dried-up river beds. Because they are so poor, the medical stuff never gets dealt with, so diseases like diabetes run their natural course and physically and mentally compromised folk remain within the family. The attitude of the family is not, 'This is a burden' but 'This is neither good nor bad, it is just how it is. God willed it and it is an honour to help unfortunate people because there but for the grace of God . . .' It is not shameful to give to beggars and they are not reviled – that is the hand life dealt them, that's all. It has long been a Moroccan custom to be politically and religiously tolerant and help the poor.

I went to the souk every day to enjoy the fascinating shops stuffed full of pyramids of spices. The vegetable shops had kumquats, limes, grapes, red onions, nutty red Moroccan potatoes, melons, pomegranates and baby pineapples. There was a hole in the wall selling precisely one bunch of mint, a basket of eggs and three packets of razor blades. I grabbed a few madeleines from a meandering tray, and checked out the medication and incense stalls selling perfumes and dyes and 'Moroccan Viagra: so good you'll be clawing up the curtains'. This led me to a rather up-market hammam where I had a good massage and wash. It was for the tourist trade: the decor was chic, it cost a lot and I would much rather have been at a cheap one, lying on the concrete floor laughing my head off with the ladies.

I had read about a restaurant called Riad Bleu Mogador and on another occasion tripped my way down narrow lanes with whitewashed houses, artisans in tiny workshops, up and down, in and out, finally getting to a dead end. As is always the case in mystical Essaouira, this turned out to be my destination. Riad Bleu is owned by one of the many expats in this town who fall in love with it, can't leave, buy a riad and set up business. In this case it was a Madame Marie-Christine Bertholet from Belgium. This was a very little riad, which had been restored delightfully and tastefully in delicate pale blue and pale green, with the dining area, little oblong shallow pool, tortoises crawling around and a fountain floating with red roses downstairs. On the first floor is the kitchen, bathroom and three bedrooms for rent, and on the top floor a salon where you could have tea and pastries. I had the choice of dining at a table in the little courtyard or in a gorgeous recessed white room with white-curtained chairs. I was seated in the Jacques Brel room, with Brel singing and me humming along, to peruse the giant white and gold tasselled menu. Brel often came to Morocco to sing and composed 'La Valse à Mille Temps' on the road from Rabat to Tangier.

The cooking was a refined mix of Moroccan and European, which Madame Bertholet called Cuisine de Soleil. Rosé was brought to me in a rose decanter with embossed Moroccan glasses, along with an amusegueule of couscous and mini vegetables served in a tiny tiny tagine dish with a teaspoon. I chose from the menu: Coupelle Craquante de Salade en Bouillabaisse aux Pistils de Safran. Although I speak fluent French, this extraordinarily florid combination of words meant nothing to me and I had no idea what I might find in front of my nostrils. I thought maybe a soup with bits of crunchy stuff, bits of things cut up and saffron somewhere. What appeared was a bowl made from crunchy pastry and filled with al dente sticks of vegetables, on top of which was a fillet of red mullet covered in a mousse-like saffron mayonnaise. It was smashing. I girded my loins and chose my next dish: Pigeonneau Laqué au Miel et Farci aux Amandes. A finger bowl with a slice of lime and a rose petal was provided so I could eat with my hands, pulling apart the pigeon and almond stuffing and transferring it to my mouth scooped up with sesame-sprinkled prunes and (bizarrely) cabbage. This was followed by an absolutely sublime chilled orange soup served in a china teacup with a silver teaspoon. Everything had been thought of; the serving dishes were silver as were all the condiment containers; the plates were beautiful and the service calm and angelic.

Previous: *Cooking sardines outside of Hôtel du Trésor*
Above: *Sardines*
Right and following: *Safi*

A few years later, on one of my recce trips to Marrakech, I mentioned to Adriano that I wanted to revisit the Essaouira I had written about in *Sirocco*. Needless to say, he had a better idea.

'No – you want to go to Safi. Don't you know about Safi?'

'Well I know it's up the coast from Essaouira and it has sardines but it's not very interesting is it? I heard it was a bit of a dump.'

Those dark Italian eyes behind black-rimmed glasses widened, which usually means he is going to impart some big wisdom to me.

'Peta – Safi is the secret new wonderful place to be. It was rather rundown but now the King has put some funds into it and it's being fixed up. It's really authentic and much more simple than Essaouira. I have bought a riad there and turned it into a hotel and I am transforming a very old and exquisite riad into an Italian cultural centre, in collaboration with the Italian government. You are going to Safi. One of my staff will drive you; you will stay the night in my hotel and my friend Majid who lives there will be your personal guide. Pack an overnight bag.'

This is Adriano all over – he knows everything and everyone and is always ready to pull a string, get an introduction or tell some risqué story about the underbelly of Marrakech. He has a completely and utterly stunningly handsome younger Moroccan boyfriend who takes him everywhere on his motorbike. Believe me, he has some stories which I wouldn't dare repeat here.

The driver and I wove through Marrakech, driving all over the place with no attachment to road rules, and with Arab music blaring on the radio. We travelled on through the red desert with its dark olive trees, to the seaside, an hour and a half away. We bumped through dry towns with dust-blown people staring at us and stopped half way at a roadside café. This large, modern, clean pit stop was a gastronomic wonderland for me. I walked past the fridges full of Coke and soft drinks, the ice creams and the snack food, and right into the slow food department out the back. A well-organised, open kitchen was cooking dozens of differing-sized tagines on their individual charcoal braziers. You ordered what you wished, it was cooked à la commande for you, and brought to the table forthwith. The favourites seemed to be fish tagines full of tomatoes, potatoes and green capsicums; or fish with cracked green olives, chermoula and lemons; or sometimes sardines with greens – a great Essaouira specialty. There were also brochettes of meat and liver grilling nearby, which you could pop into bread. The only thing missing was a cold beer and a sing-song.

The reason Safi has been ignored is not only because it was a bit run down but because of the huge, ugly phosphate factory dominating the seafront. You see it before you see the town but you shouldn't let that put you off – keep going and you will find the most charming, simple little city full of people who are honestly proud of it. I was met by handsome Majid (another handsome Moroccan) who let me into Adriano's hotel, which is a riad but completely different from a Marrakech one, mainly in its feel – it felt like a seaside house being much more casual and colourful and with absolutely no sound proofing. There were two levels above ground floor with two large bedrooms on each floor, looking out onto the port. Cute beyond endurance, the ground floor has a large salon with comfy chairs, TV, magazines and books and in the corner by the reception there is a little kitchen for the maid to make breakfasts. Walking around the truly authentic medina, I immediately felt what Adriano must have felt when he first saw the potential here. It is actually very pretty and there is NO hassling from people in the street – that's how unaccustomed they are to tourists. I really like Safi for its sweet, adorable, gentle feeling and decided that when I went back to Marrakech to film with Jane and Jeff I would convince them to come to visit and do a story on sardines. I was attracted to the huge contrast between the calm of serene Safi and the madness of manic Marrakech.

When Jeff and Jane came to Marrakech, we piled into a rented car with camera equipment and set off to get lost on the route to the Atlantic coast and Safi. We eventually got there, falling gratefully into Majid's arms, who thought it was very droll and perplexing that we took so long to arrive. Tall, slim and relaxed, he made us mint tea then we all hit the town to do our instant recce, a technique we cleverly specialise in. Where Marrakech is pink and red, Safi is blue and white – it sparkles in the sunshine and the sea air is clean. It doesn't have the wind and mist of Essaouira. It is the capital of the Doukkala-Abda region, is Morocco's main fishing port and the most important sardine port in the world. The Moroccan sardine industry nets over two billion dollars in export earnings a year and they are the best sardines in the world. It was originally, in Roman times, called Asfi, after a river, and its people were among the first Moroccans to embrace Islam. The Phoenicians were there but it was the Almohads (Berber Muslims) who really built the first colony in the twelfth century. In those times Safi was rich and an important cultural and religious centre. The Portuguese were the occupiers in the early sixteenth century and Safi's appearance owes much to their short thirty-three year legacy, with the imposing Qasr el-Bahr fortress on the foreshore (which the locals call the 'sea castle'), the Kechla fortress on the hill, the Portuguese cathedral and the ancient medina walls. By the seventeenth century Safi was enriching itself in the sugar and copper trades and the Spanish and Dutch were there, but in the following century the port at Essaouira was built and smaller Safi lost out. Then the French came around 1912 and when they left in 1956 Safi went downhill.

We were excited about hitting the port as soon as possible, so the next morning Jeff and Jane were up at the first crack of dawn and I was up at the second crack of dawn, having painted my face and put on a freshly pressed Marni dress – blue and white in homage to the colours of Safi. The fishing boats don't really start coming in until eight o'clock and continue all morning. The boats do bring in other fish and seafood but it's mostly sardines – in a good season they can bring in thirty tons of sardines a day. Fishermen in their hundreds make up this daily scene – some sardines are sold on the spot and some go to restaurants, women come down and buy sardines for their families. Fishermen are always rather ribald and there's a great air of joyousness and fun at a fishing port – it's the same in Essaouira. We filmed an extraordinary looking man: he was filthy, had a fishy jumper wrapped around his head like a turban and was busy turning octopuses inside out. When he looked up at the camera smiling and holding out an octopus to us, we saw his rugged, swashbuckling face with the most piercing blue eyes. I wondered how fragrant it would be for his wife to share a bed with a piscatorial pirate. Of course a television camera brings out the best in Moroccans and they were all making jokes about my being so dressed up at a fish market. Despite the machinations of modern commerce, it's easy to become utterly immersed in this age-old fishing ritual. Their way of plying the seas in the traditional blue, green and white wooden fishing boats is both honest and meaningful. There's a timelessness to it – generations of seafarers have hauled and gutted sardines on this very shore.

Baby Octopus Salad

Serves 6

1 kg baby octopus (or prawns)
1 bay leaf and sprigs of rosemary, sage, etc.
½ tsp salt
2 green capsicums (300 g), diced
1 onion (150 g), diced
500 g cherry tomatoes, halved
6 cloves garlic, minced
1 handful chopped fresh mint
2 tbsp lemon juice
½ a preserved lemon diced, 1 tbsp of its juice
4 tbsp extra virgin olive oil
sea salt and freshly ground black pepper
1 tsp harissa

1. Bring lots of water to boil in a large pot. Put in octopus, herbs and salt. Cover, bring to the boil (takes about 3 minutes) then immediately throw octopus into a colander to drain. Rinse with cold water.
2. If you're using prawns, peel them and remove the heads and back vein. If they're raw, dip them in boiling water for 2 minutes.
3. Toss them in with all other ingredients.

A bit of filming around the port of Safi quickly attracted the attention of the police. Jane obediently showed the permission papers but they were not accepted and we clearly had dastardly purposes up our sleeves. Off we marched to the Commissariat de Police and sat in the office trying to look normal and respectable. Majid calmly explained what we were doing but after twenty minutes, it was obvious we were getting nowhere. The sticking point was that we had permission to film in Marrakech, not in Safi. Majid pulled me aside and said, 'The chief upstairs is very partial to charming women and I am absolutely sure if you go up there, get him on his own and be suitably obsequious, we will be out of here.' Dear reader, that is exactly what happened. In fact, all the policemen in the office gathered around to tell us their favourite recipes and the way their mothers cook sardines.

Having seen the thousands of plump, juicy, silvery sardines being hauled away in crates, we were desperate to taste some so Majid took us to his favourite, rustic, foreshore sardine shack – restaurant would be too glamorous a word. There's lots of them in Safi and they are mostly simple, fun places dedicated wholly to silver fish and that great Moroccan favourite, tships. You sit outside overlooking the harbour and the sardines are cooked on grills in front of you. Inside they are making salads and cooking tships, which they love serving luke warm or cold, having little understanding of the importance of a hot, crisp shard of potato. Every time someone threatened cooking tships I made it my mission to give them some culinary hints. I wrote a whole section in one of my cookbooks on how to fry a chip, which potatoes to use and which fat. Horse fat is the best and pig lard next, but the likelihood of getting pig fat in Morocco was about equal to getting a gin and tonic at an AA meeting so I compromised with them on the fat issue. Moroccans also quite like throwing the dreaded yellow food colouring into the fat so the tships are often orange – slightly disconcerting. My real mission was to get the sardine grilling guy to co-ordinate with the tship guy in a symphony of culinary ecstasy. Majid looked on at my performance with patient, gentle tolerance and I know in my heart he thought I was an obsessive-compulsive ding-bat. Most hot countries don't serve hot food – they serve it warm.

In the meantime the table was set with cutlery, paper napkins, soft drinks, harissa, lemon wedges, bread and the familiar freshly chopped tomato, onion and green capsicum salad. The outdoor sardine shacks specialise in really crappy music – like 1950s Italian – Adriano would love it. You'll be thrilled to know we did get hot tships – amazingly delicious because of the waxy texture and nutty taste of Moroccan potatoes. This is how they cook sardines: you've got your long charcoal grill at perfect heat; you douse the unscaled, unemptied sardines with coarse, pink sea salt and place them in small, folding grills on top of the main grill; five minutes on one side, five minutes on the other and zip – onto your plate. By this time we were all hysterical with longing because once you've tasted a Moroccan sardine, you are spoiled forever. One big advantage is the fish are so fresh – if they were any fresher you'd have to slap them. There's no refrigeration needed because all the fish is sold and you just start again the next day. When I think of principal food groups I think Champagne, foie gras, caviar, Irish potatoes and Safi sardines. This is how you eat them: with your fingers, you pull the crisp skin off – they don't eat it; then you take the flesh underneath, which is incredibly sweet, tender and not strong or sardiney at all. Very, very delicate. The best fish and chips in the world.

Safi cooking is rather more refined than the rest of the country – the smen is covered in spices and herbs and the chermoula is more fragrant and has more saffron. In Safi they cook fish tagines on a bed of bamboo to prevent the delicate fish sticking. In place of bamboo you can use carrots or celery. Other specialities are fish couscous, eel with raisins, fish stuffed with freshly chopped tomatoes, rice and herbs and fish with butter, cumin and onions. They eat a lot of prawns and fish simply dusted with semolina and fried. The chermoula or marinade will be served on the side or they stuff it into the butterflied sardines, fold them over and grill them. Cooking fish stuffed with fruit or almond paste is also a speciality. Safi's most famous fish dish is Boulettes de Sardines or sardine balls in sauce – even children know how to make it.

Sardine Boulettes

Serves 6 (makes approximately 60 little boulettes)

For the boulettes:
1 kg sardine fillets or white fish fillets
freshly ground black pepper
1 tsp sea salt
½ tsp ground ginger
½ tsp paprika
½ tsp ground cumin
¼ cup parsley, chopped
¼ cup coriander, chopped
1 small onion, finely diced
½ cup cooked rice or breadcrumbs
4 tbsp lemon juice

1. Cube fish and mince in a food processor.
2. Place in a bowl and stir in all other ingredients. With wet hands, form into little balls.

For the sauce:
1 small onion, diced
2 tbsp olive oil
1 kg ripe tomatoes, chopped
1 capsicum, diced
½ cup celery leaves, chopped
2 tbsp parsley, chopped
2 cloves garlic, chopped
sea salt and freshly ground black pepper
1 tsp ground cumin
1 tsp paprika
4 pinches saffron, soaked in 1 cup boiling water for
    half an hour

To garnish:
Pink olives and lemon wedges

1. In a large saucepan or tagine dish, sauté onions in olive oil until golden. Add all other ingredients including the water saffron has been soaking in. Simmer for half an hour, until everything is soft.
2. Poach the sardine boulettes in the sauce for 10 minutes.
   Serve in shallow bowls with pink olives, lemon wedges and chunks of bread.

Many famous fish tagine recipes come from Safi also.

Tagine of Fish and Preserved Lemon

Serves 6

For the chermoula:
1 cup flat leaf parsley, chopped
1 cup coriander, chopped
1 preserved lemon
4 cloves garlic, crushed
2 tsp hot smoked paprika
2 tsp ground cumin
2 generous pinches saffron, soaked for 10 minutes in 2 tbsp boiling water
1 tsp ground ginger
½ tsp salt

For the tagine:
1.2 kg firm-fleshed white fish
2 large green capsicums
300 g ripe, acid free or Roma tomatoes
300 g waxy potatoes
6 x 10-cm pieces of bamboo or 6 bamboo chopsticks
1 medium-sized tagine dish or oven dish
2 cloves garlic
3 tbsp extra virgin olive oil
1 heaped tbsp sliced almonds and coriander for garnish

1. To make chermoula marinade, place the parsley, coriander, flesh of the preserved lemon and garlic in a mortar and pestle and smash together or blend in the food processor. Place this paste in a bowl and add spices, including the saffron water.
2. Cut fish into six portions, rub the chermoula all over and let stand for half an hour.
3. Quarter capsicums, core and remove seeds. Peel and quarter tomatoes. Peel and slice potatoes thinly. Slice preserved lemon skin.
4. Criss-cross bamboo on the bottom of the tagine. Place fish covered in chermoula on top, then potatoes, preserved lemon, tomatoes and garlic. Form a pyramid shape. Pour over olive oil.
5. Bake at 180 °C (355 °F) or simmer on stove top for 45 minutes. Serve sprinkled with grilled sliced almonds and fresh coriander.

Majid loves Safi with a passion and is happy that new life is being breathed into it because he wants to share it with visitors. He would like everyone to know how special it is with its history, monuments, medina and fabulous seafood. A lot of development money is finally being poured into the town, the ugly phosphate factory will be moved outside the centre and everything is being done up. An excellent example of the construction going on is the renovation of the old spice market. This is a very pretty indoor market with a central area and little shops all around the sides. Everything was being painted blue and white. There are markets like this specialising in different foods all over Safi. Majid took us to a harsha shop. Harsha is a semolina griddle bread that doesn't require yeast. Years ago in Kenitra I sat down at a seaside café and watched a young woman making a large semolina flat bread and found out what it was called. She made the mixture by throwing a whole lot of semolina into a large bowl, adding some vegetable oil, vanilla, salt and warm water, and mixing it up with her hands. Then she heated some oil in a black pan 40 centimetres across and poured the mixture in, leaving it to cook for about twenty minutes. She made a hole in the centre with her finger so it wouldn't blow up, and every so often poked other little holes to let air out. To turn it she inverted it onto a wooden tray, then slid it back in to cook on the other side. Golden triangles of it were wrapped in paper and sold to the ravenous hoards. This is very similar to what they make in Spain, in fact when I was on a beach in Tangier a man was wandering around selling calientes, a flat semolina cake made with olive oil and egg similar to harsha and seemingly of Spanish/Jewish origin. He carried it around in a large, flat, aluminium pan with an ornate lid that folded out half way to expose the golden bread, which he cut off in pointed slices. The harsha shop in the Safi medina is famous, tiny and full of friendly, chirpy women selling the yellow, crunchy, delicious bread.

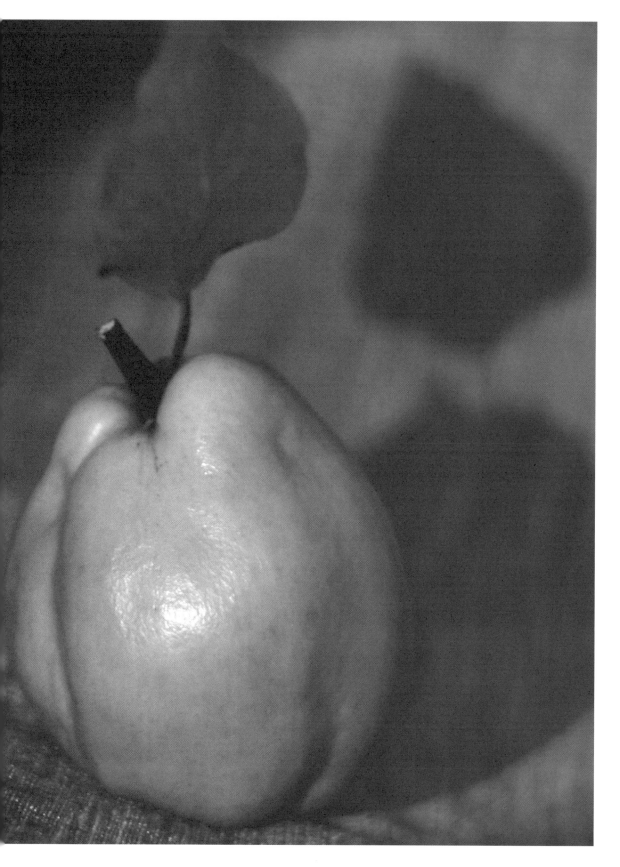

The gastronomads didn't come to Safi so we brought Safi to Hôtel du Trésor in Marrakech. For our sardine and salad cooking class I got Amina to share her knowledge with us. A lot of the male staff at Hôtel du Trésor are from Safi so they were very excited to be diving into their adored sardines. First we hit the mellah and Amina ordered lots of sardines. We bought the ingredients for our salads plus anything else we liked the look of. When the fish was prepped and the salads chopped, Amina set up a little charcoal barbecue outside in the alley. Ten minutes later we were sitting by the pool, combining sardines with rosé, as only a serious cooking class can.

Marinated Sardines

Serves 6

½ cup lemon juice
6 small garlic cloves, crushed
1 tsp sea salt
freshly ground black pepper
½ tsp ground cumin
1 tsp paprika
2 tbsp olive oil
36 fresh sardines

1. Mix all ingredients aside from sardines together in a large bowl.
2. Gut sardines and remove backbones and heads. You can ask your fishmonger to do this for you. Place in a large bowl of water and wash, rubbing off scales.
3. Now drench all sardines in the marinade. Grill on barbecue in a folding grill for a few minutes on each side.

Carrot and Orange Blossom Salad

Serves 4–6

500 g carrots
2 oranges
½ cup fresh orange juice
juice of 1 lemon
2 tbsp orange blossom water
1 tbsp caster sugar
½ tsp sea salt
ground cinnamon

1. Peel carrots and grate into long strands.
2. Peel oranges. Remove pips and pith and cut flesh into cubes. Add to carrots.
3. Mix together juices, orange blossom water, sugar and salt. Pour over carrots and oranges.

Wind into mounds on the plate with a fork and sprinkle with cinnamon.

Tchaktchouka is a very popular tomato and capsicum salad found all over North Africa. It resembles Spanish gazpacho and quite clearly has Andalusian influence. It has many variations and I give two here. The first one is the raw one, common in Safi. The second one takes advantage of Moroccans' love of mixing textures – this one has grilled capsicums with raw tomatoes but sometimes it is made the other way round. I find it heavenly. Moroccans usually peel tomatoes for a salad, even if it's for a raw one.

Tchaktchouka
Tomato, Onion and Green Capsicum Salad

Serves 4–6

500 g ripe Roma or acid free tomatoes
2 large green capsicums
1 medium white onion
2 cloves garlic
sea salt and freshly ground pepper
3 tbsp extra virgin olive oil
2 tbsp lemon juice or white vinegar
chilli flakes, optional

1. Peel, deseed and dice tomatoes.
2. Core, deseed and dice capsicums.
3. Dice onion and chop garlic.
4. Mix together in a bowl with salt, pepper, oil, lemon juice or vinegar and chilli, if wished.

Tomato and Red Capsicum Salad

Serves 4–6

2 large red capsicums, charred, peeled and seeded
500 g acid free or Roma tomatoes, peeled and deseeded
½ a preserved lemon, 1 tsp of the juice
2 tbsp coriander, chopped
½ tsp ground cumin
½ tsp sea salt
freshly ground black pepper to taste
1 tbsp olive oil

1. Dice in big pieces the capsicums and tomatoes and place in a bowl.
2. Remove flesh from lemon and discard. Wash rind and dice finely. Add to the bowl along with the juice.
3. Add other ingredients. Mix well and serve at room temperature.

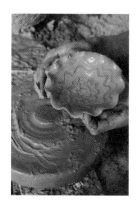

Adorable, gentle Safi is famous for another thing – its pottery. The beehive-shaped kilns and the pottery workshops look like they're part of the hills – like they've just risen up from the surrounding clay. Inside what amounts to a cave, I'm introduced to one of Safi's master potters hard at work. Our filmed visit prompts a frenzied burst of production. A baby tagine, roof tiles, water jugs, plates, vases, an ashtray – it goes on. Outside in the hot sun, the pots are set to harden and when there's an ample supply the kilns are fired up with wood. Then, in another cave, the painting takes place with time-honoured designs practised to perfection. And then much of the pottery is sent all over Morocco to market. When you have been in places like Moulay Idriss you see the beautiful covering on the roofs, made out of green tiles. Safi is the place where these are produced. Safi pottery is considered by some to be the most refined in Morocco because they have had centuries to practise. It has a particular look which comes from Andalusia – shiny, almost metallic-looking and multicoloured. They use arabesques (Moorish/Andalusian ornate, intertwined, geometric painting) and beautiful glazing. You often see fish on the more modern designs.

My first visit to a pottery was in Fès, where there is an association with the Safi style of design. The guide turned up first thing in the morning, smartly combed and dressed in cream bloomers, bleached shirt, pale blue jellaba, white socks and cream shoes. We visitors fell in behind obediently. Our first stop was in fact fascinating – a pottery and tile factory just outside town. The clay was softened by foot by a man who spent all day barefoot stamping great lumps of it into a big thick circle. He then cut this circle up into large portions and recommenced his stamping of it. This he did three times, then it was ready for the potters or the tilers. Behind him was a mountain of waiting clay, and to the side the ever-present mint tea setup. In the same dim room, the potters were quietly working away throwing their pots. The tilers cut the clay up into squares and laid them out in the sun to dry. The ovens were built of clay and stones (with the occasional pot stuck into the wall for luck) and fired with olive wood and the leftovers from olive pressings. This smoke was black because of the olives but apparently clean. The first firing in a beehive-shaped oven was at 600 °C (approximately 1200 °F) for nine hours; the second firing at the same temperature was in a cave-like oven.

After the pots had been washed with lime, they went to the painting room. This is the best job, in my opinion, but women are not allowed to do it. Seven men and seven pots of mint tea lined this light-filled room. They were surrounded by little bowls of different coloured paint and each painter marked each pot on the back with his finger. Blue is the colour of Fès and the cobalt glaze responsible for the colour of the pottery comes from a process developed in the tenth century. In the mosaic room we found men gently tapping out tiny mosaics with chisels. To make a large zellij panel, each differently shaped and coloured bit is individually stuck on in complex, traditional patterns – an enormous and painstaking labour of love. The tradition of zellij came from Byzantium and was influenced by Moorish Spain. Moroccan mosaics are flamboyantly colourful and rely on a complex mathematical geometry for artistic expression. There are more than 360 fourmah shapes for the zlayiyyah craftsman to memorise in this spectacular geometrical art, which covers mosques, palaces and public buildings all over Morocco.

Now, as we are at the seaside, I have to talk to you about beaches and foreigners in Morocco. The beach at Safi is one of the most famous surf beaches in the world, the most beautiful one being Lalla Fatna, about 12 kilometres along the road. There are big surfing competitions here and the place is taken over by blond-haired, white-lipped men in board shorts. As you may well imagine, going to the beach in Morocco is fraught, keeping in mind the suppression of women. My first beach experience in the north of Morocco involved everything I love most: throngs of humanity, hundreds of young males taking up the best stretch of the beach right next to the water with ball games, camels, children kicking sand in your eyes, and best of all, an oil spill that left black tar sticking to our bodies. It was on you before you even realised it was in the sea, and the more you rubbed it off, the more you spread it.

My next experience was at Merkala Beach, also known as Jews' River, in Tangier and involved my friend Jonathan and Mr Lhascen, whom we met in Chapter Four. Jonathan's car bumped along a dirt track, at the end of which he assured my friend and I we would find Spain. And that's exactly what we found. This beach is at the tip of Morocco and you can see Andalusia and the Rock of Gibraltar across the narrow strait. The mild waves signalled to us that we were exactly at the meeting place of the Atlantic Ocean and the Mediterranean Sea. We plonked ourselves down with towels, baskets and sun block, and took our clothes off to reveal various styles of swimwear. This caused an intake of breath that swept the entire beach of unalloyed Moroccan composition. We were the only Europeans and the only women in swimsuits. Moroccan girls up to puberty wear swimsuits and even two pieces and pretty, fashionable clothes but the minute they reach a certain age, their life of freedom is over. All older girls and women on the beach and in the water were fully dressed in jellaba, some even with scarves. Boys and men wore swimsuits because apparently their bodies do not provoke thoughts of lust. Nevertheless, I can report young Moroccan men are very good-looking, with slim, well-proportioned bodies and fine bone structures – eminently lust-provoking. I have no idea what the women look like, but their faces are often beautiful and they have strong, healthy hair. Jonathan discreetly poured us all glasses of rosé and we swam and sunbathed, talking and laughing with the other men of David's household and his friends from the beach. All the while Jonathan's homme à tout faire Mr Lhascen stared adoringly at my friend.

'Mr Lhascen, stop making eyes at Madame,' Jonathan admonished, refilling his glass.

'I can't help it. I think I must ask her to marry me. She is too beautiful. Ah, but I have no money. . . she not marry me.'

'That's right, you old fool. Why would she marry you – you don't even have any teeth.' Then to me, 'You know he was a very handsome man in his youth and had many women. I've bought this man three sets of teeth and he's sold them all. I even have to watch the silver. I think he's got a Georgian silverware shop somewhere in the medina, entirely stocked with the contents of my flat.'

We were a source of unflagging attention and by now a circle of children and young people had formed around us. They lay on their bellies, supporting their chins in their hands and stared quietly as if we were a television set. I gave three little girls my lipstick and mirror, which they took back to show their veiled older sisters. They presently gave them back, having examined them closely but not applied them.

'Peta,' Jonathan said, 'you have at least six marriage proposals from these Adonises surrounding us. They think you're the most glamorous thing they've ever seen and are convinced you are very rich. It's up to you to choose which one you would like. I can't introduce any of my European friends to my Moroccan male friends because they fall for each other immediately and I never see either of them again. I've lost two of my cooks to visiting women. Whisked them off to Australia, for heaven's sake.'

Frankly, I wasn't thinking marriage, but when in Rome. . .

Behind us on a raised, rocky part of the beach was a row of ramshackle little stalls selling tagines, fresh pears and watermelons, kef (hashish) and hot and cold drinks. No alcohol but everyone was stoned. We drank iwiza, which is mint tea made with lemon verbena, then all piled into the car, an action which provoked loud, insistent chanting from one of the stalls.

'What is wrong with that man?' I asked Jonathan.

'Nothing. He's singing the praises of your bottom.'

'Oh,' I smiled. 'How kind.' Only in Morocco are the curves you so assiduously try to get rid of praised.

'You see, Peta, there is no youth culture here in Morocco. All women of all shapes and ages are beautiful and seducible. Also they have no concept of time, and age is time, so age is not an issue and neither is sex. They would happily go with people of the same sex and not consider themselves homosexual at all.'

This is an interesting thing about Moroccan male sexuality. There are lots of men who are heterosexual and quite happily sleep with the same sex occasionally and don't consider themselves to be gay; don't consider themselves to be anything; they consider themselves to be just sexual. It's not talked about much, but it is very common. They believe that this is the norm and don't really adhere to the idea that they may be part of a minority. They don't get the concept of gay because they think it is completely normal to express sexual interest in both sexes. They consider it masculine to show affection, hold hands and be physically intimate with their male friends. Anthropological research has suggested that in Afghanistan, India, Pakistan, Bangladesh, Sri Lanka, Morocco and elsewhere, men's sexual desires for other men is understood as mainstream. This thinking predates Western ideas of sexuality and gender and it has even been suggested that the whole concept of homosexuality is quite recent. Before the mid-nineteenth century when the words 'homosexual' and 'sexual orientation' began to be used, homosexuality did not exist as a separate notion. There is also the possibility that Moroccan men go for other men when they are younger or before marriage because they are unable to sleep with the women before marriage.

Chapter Six
Mint Tea & Nectarome

Marrakech is a city of well over a million people where contrast reigns supreme. Subsistence workers and their donkey carts juxtapose with flashy international brands and the smell of money. There are two distinct lives: the traditional, colourful, overcrowded life of the medina and the new, calm, more chic life of the Guéliz or French quarter. It's a half hour walk to a different world – here the boulevards are wide and clean, the restaurants charge Paris prices, it's party party party and there's absolutely no problem getting a drink, an expensive hairdresser or French perfume. There are posh, expensive suburbs with exclusive apartment buildings fronted by well-watered lawns and well-fed guardians. I love the madness of the medina (even though it does drive me to colourful adjectives at times) but there are some great places in the Guéliz. One is the Sky Bar at the elegant, arty Bab Hotel with its pool, white pebbles underfoot and terrifyingly mini-skirted waitresses. It's hard to believe you're actually in Marrakech.

Café de la Poste looks colonial on the outside but is a modern Parisian-style brasserie on the inside. This is where the m'as-tu-vu (show-off) crowd go. It's a great place to meet friends, flirt and eat expensive but not particularly stunning Mediterranean-style food.

Comptoir bar/restaurant is very fashionable and cool and lots of fun, if a bit noisy. The restaurant downstairs is not bad and in the evening they have a fabulous floor and table-top show of belly dancing and traditional Berber dancing of women balancing many candles on a plate on their heads. But the real place to be is at the bar upstairs where famous folk, wealthy foreign businessmen and high-class Russian call girls vie for cocktail space. If you ever see an unattractive older man with a drop-dead young beauty sitting at the same table in Marrakech, you know what the deal is.

La Mamounia is a very old and famous, recently renovated five star hotel. The decor is a sumptuous combination of art deco and Moroccan, complete with fountains with roses floating in them, chandeliers the size of small cottages, designer and antique shops, casino and dark jazzy piano bar. It was originally built in an olive grove within the ancient imperial capital. On my first visit I walked outside to the lovely gardens, which appear to go on for ever, ignored the sign that said 'Swimming pool – only guests beyond this point' and quietly bristled at the rich, fat, ugly people lying around the pool. Huge high olive trees stand among orange, fig and pomegranate trees with fruit hanging from their branches. Succulents and delicate blossoms are everywhere. Back at the bar I had a moment of madness and ordered a kir, which set me back 300 dirham, more than the price of a room in the medina. I could have ridden around on a bloody camel for a week at that price. It's true that La Mamounia is fabulous but it's quite removed from the action, both culturally and physically.

The Majorelle Gardens were originally constructed by the French painter Jacques Majorelle, the property later being bought by Yves Saint-Laurent. It is very beautiful and peaceful with fountains, cactus, bamboo and palms. A villa painted the most incredible, intense blue is hugged by cerise bougainvillea.

Al Fassia is to my mind the best restaurant in Marrakech. It serves Fassi (from Fès) food and is staffed entirely by women. I discovered Siroua wine at Al Fassia restaurant. Most Moroccan wine is produced from the rich soil in the triangle of Kenitra, Fès and Meknes and Safi, as is most olive oil. There is also some production south of Casablanca, constituting about 60,000 hectares in all. Well, actually, there are technically about fourteen different growing districts. The French put down the first vines at the beginning of the century, instituted their appellation system but didn't stay long enough to make sure that standards were kept up. Most people in Morocco drink rosé or gris, which is eminently suited to the climate and the spicy food, but it's exciting to sup on a good red with the thick, rich tagines. To tell the truth, it's so hard to get a drink in the medina, you'd be grateful to get anything – once or twice I looked longingly at trucks with petrol leaks and thought, If I could just lie under that truck and have a good sniff. . . Gerouane and Beni M'Tir are commonly drunk wines which are okay – they're sturdy and go well with the aromatic food. Cuvée du President is found on most restaurant menus. I like Siroua Syrah the best for its rich, smooth, slightly plumy-spicy taste.

Top left: *Mohamed*
Bottom left: *Dining chez Mohamed*

Towards the end of our culinary adventure, slightly slowed down by our week-long dinner party, we took the gastronomads out into the bled again, to chill out and smell the roses. Nectarome is an organic garden complex set in the enchanting Ourika Valley, about forty-five minutes south of Marrakech. The Ourika is one of the most spectacular and beautiful valleys in the foothills of the Atlas Mountains, carpeted with emerald fields and wonderful gardens. You drive through the village of Tnine Ourika and enter Nectarome by a big gate. The smiling guide, Ilham, meets you. Nectarome is based in an organic aromatic garden and is designed so visitors can experience the fifty plants and herbs used in the company's wellness products. The complex also helps sustain the local area by recruiting workers from the local village. Thanks to their hard work, we're all overcome with gladness at the delicious scents of mints, thymes, geraniums, basils, flowers and such like. Our beautiful and knowledgeable guide has everyone swooning, and also taking on board the medicinal uses of the regional plants like tensi, which regulates blood pressure.

This place is absolutely magical and wonderful because it's full of herbs that a lot of us grow in our gardens but we've forgotten what their medicinal uses are. In medieval times everybody knew why they had rosemary in the garden – because it was good for digestion. People knew they had lavender because it is a calmant and also very good for your hair. We like the exotic taste of cumin but don't know that it stops nausea. Getting sick is something that occasionally happens in Morocco

and you need to know about cumin. It was in the middle of the medina that I first got that lonely feeling – like grief but physical. No one can help you, no one can stop you, nothing can reverse it, and Moroccan law stipulates that you will be three kilometres from a toilet when it happens. Bombay Bottom, Deli Belly, Rabat Rumbles, Moroccan Mambo – the dance everyone warned me I would eventually have to do. Panic stricken, I ran around in circles asking for a pharmacy or a toilet, whichever took the shortest time. I found a pharmacy, bought the pills to stop the lonely feeling, and waited patiently for relief. To recover I bought anything I could that smelled nice, like dried rosebuds and pink and white flowers from the oleander trees. It was while I was buying the fragrant smelling things that a man told me about cumin. It tastes horrible to eat but it works.

Another thing which grows at Nectarome is the henna plant – used as a dye for hair, skin and fingernails, as a dye and preservative for leather and cloth, and as an anti-fungal. It is applied as part of a special celebration normally and signifies beauty, luck and joy. Henna painting is not originally Moroccan – it comes from India and has moved through the Middle Eastern and Arab world. Commercially available henna powder is made by drying the henna leaves and milling them to powder, which is then sifted. This powder is mixed with lemon juice, strong tea, or other mildly acidic liquids. Essential oils such as tea tree, eucalyptus or lavender will improve the stain. The ingredient in henna leaves which produces the stain is called lawsone and it must be activated – if you crush henna leaves in your hand, it won't stain. When the henna is broken down, powdered and mixed with fluid, cellulose in the leaf is dissolved and the lawsone starts acting – the longer you leave the paste on your skin or in your hair, the deeper the red stain will be. They say it should stay on for at least six hours but you'd have to be Moroccan or stoned to stay still for that long. The design is applied to your hands or feet and when it has fallen off the skin or been removed by scraping, the stain will be orange, but will darken over the following three days to a reddish brown. After the stain reaches its peak colour it will appear to fade. The henna stain is not actually fading, the skin is exfoliating. The lower, less stained cells, rise to the surface, until all stained cells are shed. If your henna design is still pale after a few days, the henna was of poor quality.

There are girls in the Djemaa el Fna Square who do it but it's much better to have it applied at home by someone who is recommended. I made friends with a family the first time I visited Morocco and they got a professional wedding henna painter in to transform me into a person who not only had brown freckles and red hair but also brown/red swirls. She sat me down on the family's breathtakingly expensive banquettes in their salon and got out her syringe and plastic bag of henna paste mixed with water and alcohol. She sucked up some paste in the syringe and set to doing a very intricate, lacy pattern on my feet. A solid layer of it was painted onto my soles and the lot dabbed with a lemon and sugar solution. It was at about that time they mentioned that it took at least two hours to set. Lunch came, and still I sat with my feet poking out like a chicken and stinging like hell from the alcohol. Boredom with the henna-drying performance set in, so I decided to somehow get my feet into my sandals, my body into my swimsuit and both parts up onto the roof to dry in the sun. The design got a bit squashed in my sandals and bits dropped off on the way up, but the mission was accomplished surprisingly successfully. I lay there for two hours, by which time my feet were set solid and it took ages to get the dried paste off in the shower. But the result! There I was, resplendent in dark red curls and dots and lacy bits up to my ankles, and solid apricot soles. I was entirely thrilled with myself and thought, One more cooking lesson on the floor, a few more hammams and I could go completely native, darling.

On another occasion my friend Fouzia arranged for me to get my hands and feet hennaed so I would leave Morocco with good memories and beautiful feet. I was wearing a modest mid-calf-length dress, but when I put my foot up on a stool to be painted she covered my knees with a cloth in case her father saw them. To while the time away I watched a video of the son's wedding. The video was like all wedding videos ever made in the history of the universe: badly needed editing. Once again I found myself covered in wet, delicate henna swirls just as lunch was served, but by the time we had ingested the delectable feast, I was dry enough to get on the train back to Casablanca. They covered my hands and feet with cotton wool for protection and instructed me to just rub the dry henna off when I got back. No one on the train thought it remotely surprising to see a woman sitting bolt upright in first class with cotton wool stuck all over her. In Marrakech I arranged for the gastronomads to get hennaed with varying results. One thing you have to be very careful of is what they call 'black henna'. There is no such thing as black henna or white henna or any other colour for that matter – real henna can only be a rich red/brown. What they call black henna has a toxic element in it called phenylenediamine, which can cause severe allergic reactions and permanent scarring.

Ilham at Nectarome told us she now only uses plants instead of chemical medicines in her home and has taught her whole family about herbs and how to use them. There are herbs at Nectarome that I don't see much of at home nowadays, but that take me right back to my chefing days in Paris, like sarriette or savory, which the French use a lot in their cooking. David says he makes an omelette with it but we tend not to use it very much. It smells absolutely beautiful and I think it would be good with chicken because it smells like a cross between rosemary and thyme. Nectarome creates and markets essential oils, herbal infusions and beauty products, using traditional Moroccan wisdom as a starting point. The herbs and flowers and trees we see are for display and education. The real growing goes on somewhere else as they need great quantities of plants to get an essential oil, for example, five thousand rose petals give just one litre.

Nectarome make all sorts of teas and herbal infusions, including the ubiquitous mint tea. English traders introduced Moroccans to tea in the nineteenth century and they immediately improved it with mint. Before that they drank mint, verbena and marjoram with hot water but as soon as tea turned up, they cleverly incorporated it into their traditional infusion. Mint tea is all over the medina, in every home and in every corner of every street you see men with their little set-up of low table and the gear for making tea. If you are negotiating for something in a shop, the transaction is smoothed by the offer of mint tea. Moroccans say they drink so much of it because the mint and sugar are cooling in the heat. Also it doesn't always smell too fragrant in the medina so the scent of mint tea is soothing. Tea is always served in little ornate glasses, not cups and quite often has orange blossoms added to it. There's nothing casual about the making of it in Morocco – if they can turn something into a ceremony, they will.

The first time I was given mint tea, the making went like this: put green gunpowder China tea in an ornate teapot, pour a glass of hot water in and pour it out again – this washes the tea. Put huge amounts of sugar in. Pick a big bunch of mint from the garden and stuff as much as you possibly can in. The mint is sort of folded and crushed as it goes in to release its flavour. The pot is now filled with water and put on the flame to boil. A glass of tea is poured and tasted then poured back in again. Now it is ready to serve. The tea is poured into little ornate glasses from on high, so bubbles are produced on the surface – this supposedly represents the circle of a Fès hat. Nothing worse than a flat glass of tea, according to Moroccans. When we filmed Amine making it at Hôtel du Trésor he seemed to pour things in and out about three times until he was satisfied and he also used a bit of absinthe. There is something exotic but familiar about sipping mint tea – you feel at home and it helps you to slip back into the slowness of the culture. It takes time to make a proper pot of mint tea so when someone offers it to you, it is an honour.

Mint Tea

Serves 6 people

large bunch of fresh mint
the most fabulous, ornate silver teapot you can find
2 tsp Chinese green tea
6 tsp sugar

1. Wash the mint. Heat the teapot with boiling water then pour it out.
2. Put in the tea and pour in a cup of boiling water. Then pour it out, leaving the washed tea in.
3. Twist and break the mint up as you put it in the teapot. Add the sugar and then fill the pot with boiling water.
4. Leave to steep for three minutes, stir then pour out one glass. Taste it for sugar and add more if you want. Pour the glass back in again – this ensures everything is blended in.
5. Pour into little ornate glasses from a height so you get bubbles on the top.

Nectarome use several vegetable oils, like almond, sesame, walnut and sunflower, but the really special and unique one is the indigenous argan oil. A great gastronomic delicacy, it is extracted from the almond-shaped kernel contained in the stone of the argan tree fruit. This nutty-tasting and smelling oil is pressed for demonstration in a large, colourful tent with mattresses around the edge. We lie around on the mattresses and watch with fascination. One woman roasts the nuts over a fire and another grinds them by hand with a small stone grinder composed of two heavy stones on top of each other. There is a hole in the top stone into which she puts the nuts then laboriously turns the stone with a handle and out comes a thick paste which looks like peanut butter. She grinds only nuts – no added water. When there's lots of paste in her bowl she then begins manipulating it with her hands and adding water. It separates into hard paste and honey/amber-coloured oil right in front of your eyes. Magical. The roasted oil is used to cook with and there is also an unroasted version used for body oil. When I put it on my skin I have the feeling I smell like a walking peanut butter sandwich. The oil, rich in vitamin E and essential fatty acids, heals and moisturises skin and is good for nails and hair. When we put our fingers in the bowl to taste, we are treated to an absolutely gorgeous nutty, roasty flavour. Argan is the third ingredient in a very good spread called amalou, comprising almonds and honey. Berbers use it for its nutty, slightly sharp flavour in couscous, tagines, with fish, in salads or dribbled on bread. As with olive oil, it is best consumed within the year.

Along with other ancient giants of food like olives, dates and grapes, argan trees can live for centuries and have very high ecological, economic and social value. Unfortunately goats and sheep adore argan leaves, and in their desperation to get at them actually jump onto the trees, reaching even the top and eating leaves, branches and new shoots. A co-operative has been created by the women of Tamanar, which is half way between Essaouira and Agadir, to protect the trees and process the nuts. It is called Amal, which in Arabic means hope. They get around the goat problem by feeding them with the leaves and pulp of the pressed fruit; the shells are used as fuel and rejected kernels are fed to livestock. Like dates, the fruit is picked in a frenzy over two months, the income supporting the growers for the rest of the year. The dried fruit is bought from local markets every two weeks, dried again, put in the pulping machine, cleaned and checked by the women. The 'nuts' are then opened by hand by whacking them with a stone on stone, which splits them, then they are roasted in a gas roaster, left overnight to cool and transferred to the press. The resulting oil is filtered and bottled, and nitrogen added to prevent oxidation.

Another wonderful, relaxing thing you can do at Nectarome is the old foot bath and massage scenario. You sit with your feet and lower legs in a tub of hot water and special salts for about thirty minutes, then lie down for a foot massage. Needless to say there is a shop full of oils, creams, teas, shampoos, soaps, face masks and all sorts of luxuries you can't do without. Just when you think you're getting a bit peckish, you are led to a beautifully set table in the middle of the garden with singing birds to be fed lunch, which is an exercise in traditional Moroccan abundance, of course. The ladies carry the trays of food from the kitchen to the table on their heads. All the vegetables, salads, fruit and herbs are grown at Nectarome, the couscous is made from barley with turnips and turnip leaves and the tagine is made with chicken, peas, broad beans and argan oil – completely delicious.

Down the road from Nectarome in Ourika is La Safranière Tnin de l'Ourika, but there is no point in going unless you can do it in the first three weeks of November. That's when the mauve saffron crocuses are flowering and you can observe the ladies working. It is very charming walking in to the property as all the discarded purple crocus flowers are lining the pathways in thick magenta decoration. Included in the visit is a tour of the saffron gardens and other herbs and trees growing on the property, watching the girls getting the pistils out, quick-drying in the kiln, buying saffron and having a cup of herbal tea. People who grow this spice say that living with saffron is like living with a demanding, seductive mistress: at times you curse her but you can't leave her for she has no substitute.

Originally brought in from Kashmir and Nepal with the Arabian traders in the ninth century, the best saffron in Morocco is grown in the Alpine town of Tailiouine, high up in the Atlas Mountains, also famous for its gemstone deposits, date palms and squadrons of pink flamingos in the winter. Tailiouine saffron is highly reputed, not only for its intense colour but also for its aromatic qualities. The purple *Crocus sativus*, from which women retrieve the bright orange stigmas (three to a crocus), flowers in autumn and sleeps in summer. The flowers open up in the pre-dawn darkness, allowing the red light of sunrise to shine on a purple carpet of flowers. They are picked by hand before dawn – back-breaking work as the crocuses grow close to the ground – then the styluses (the stalks connecting stigmas to the host crocus flower) are delicately removed to be dried in wooden boxes. Overnight, as if by magic, the flowers grow again, the bare field becomes purple and you start collecting anew at dawn. You need 18,000 to 20,000 flowers to obtain one kilo of saffron – that's 140,000 styluses.

The method of drying is very important in establishing the unique aroma. Eastern saffron is sun-dried, bringing out very spicy notes and western saffron is dried by artificial heat, which develops an intense saffron flavour. For the consumer in Morocco, this golden spice costs 10–12 dirham per gram, half the price of the Spanish product and a fifth of the price you would pay in America. Morocco produces about two tons yearly. In the Middle Ages, saffron was used to dye wedding-night sheets pale yellow, to make disappearing ink, as an anti-spasmodic medication and as an aphrodisiac. Myth has it that one day Zeus decided to make love on a bed of saffron, having wound lotus and jasmine in his lover's hair. Its glorious reddish orange colour is considered to be holy in Tibet and it not only dyes food but also cloth in Asia – not to mention you and your clothes, if you get it on yourself. Today Moroccans use it not only for cooking, both savoury and sweet, but also in mint tea, as a rheumatism drug and for eye make-up.

Saffron is the most expensive spice in the world – priced higher than gold – but a little goes a long way and the exotic, musky smell is incomparable. There is much cheating in the saffron trade. The thing they usually stretch it with is dyed corn beard or safflower stamens. It is almost impossible to tell the difference until you cook with it, because it looks and smells the same. If it is powdered it could be turmeric, which is delicious but it's not saffron. Saffron that you have bought cheaply is obviously not the real thing, but sometimes the price is just high enough to lull you into security. I bought a whole lot at the souk. It was wrapped in little pieces of newspaper, and when I got home I threw a whole teaspoonful in a tagine. Normally this would have ruined it, as only a few styluses are needed to give out the pungent, earthy flavour, but my 'saffron' neither coloured nor flavoured the dish. In the Middle Ages, saffron fraudsters were burnt alive in the town square: I think it would be reasonable to bring that colourful custom back. Saffron is too expensive for most Moroccans to buy but they love the bright yellow colour it turns their tagines, so they use the cheap colorant alimentaire, which is carcinogenic. I don't think they know this as they use it with alacrity.

When Moroccans say salad, they normally mean a cooked salad which is served at room temperature. Variations of green capsicum and tomato salads are very common and bear an obvious resemblance to the gazpachos of Andalusia. In Arabic, gazpacho means soaked bread. The Spanish got the idea from the Moors who made it out of bread, water, olive oil, lemon juice, garlic and salt. The Moors left Spain at about the time that Columbus came back from America, bringing with him capsicums and tomatoes. So these vegetables got thrown into the gazpacho and went back across the water to Morocco to be converted into salads. I particularly liked the texture combinations where raw tomatoes are combined with cooked capsicums or the other way round.

At a meal, depending on how formal it is, you could have anything from three to fifteen little plates mostly made up of vegetables. The spiced or sweetened flavours are divinely balanced and can be prepared in advance.

You could get:
- Grilled red capsicums with preserved lemon
- Tomato jam
- Okra with tomatoes
- Fried chopped liver
- Grated cucumber and mint
- Sweet puréed pumpkin with sesame seeds
- Eggplant salad
- Sliced, grilled eggplant stuffed with almond paste
- Green capsicum and tomato salad
- Marinated olives
- Grated beetroot with cinnamon and parsley
- Cooked courgettes with za'atar (combination of thyme, marjoram and oregano)
- Artichoke hearts
- Carrots with oranges and orange blossom water
- Chickpeas and broad beans with spices and herbs
- Lamb's brains with garlic and coriander
- Anchovies and olives
- Chopped fresh lemon with parsley and onion
- Stewed white beans
- Cubed potatoes with mint
- Lentils with saffron rice
- Bread

Broad Bean Salad

Serves 6 as a starter

1.5 kg fresh broad beans or 500 g frozen
2 tbsp olive oil
1 small onion, finely chopped
2 cloves garlic, finely chopped
½ tsp cumin seeds
½ tsp sea salt
juice of 1 lime
2 tbsp mint or flat leaf parsley, chopped

1. If fresh, remove beans from pods. Plunge into salted, boiling water for three minutes. Drain and run cold water over them to keep green colour. Remove outer skins. Follow the same process if using frozen beans.

2. Heat oil in a fry pan and sauté the onion, garlic and cumin for a few minutes until golden. Add the beans and salt. Quickly heat through. Place the bean mixture into a bowl, pour over the lime juice and toss in mint or parsley.

Gården Hërb Şálád

lemon juice

extra virgin olive oil

1 shallot, finely chopped

Dijon mustard

sea salt

freshly ground black pepper

mixed salad leaves

mixture of garden herbs like mint, coriander, parsley, basil,
   chives, tarragon, savory, dill, lemon balm, chervil

mixture of salad flowers like calendula, cornflower,
   marigold, nasturtium, pansy, verbena and herb flowers,
   e.g. basil and rosemary

1. Make up vinaigrette of one part lemon juice to two parts olive oil,
   shallot, a little mustard, salt and pepper. Whisk together.
2. Wash and dry salad leaves, herbs and flowers. Toss with just
   enough vinaigrette to cover leaves and serve immediately.

Zaahlouk
Eggplant Salad

Serves 4–6 as a starter

2 very ripe medium-sized tomatoes
500 g eggplants
olive oil
4 cloves garlic, finely chopped
½ tsp ground cumin
½ tsp paprika
2 tbsp lemon juice
sea salt and freshly ground black pepper
1 tbsp coriander, finely chopped
1 tsp parsley, finely chopped

1. Peel, seed and chop tomatoes.
2. Peel strips off eggplants so they are striped. Slice in 1.5-cm rounds. At this point, most recipes say to salt them but eggplants these days are bred not to be bitter, so I skip that part.
3. Fry eggplant slices in a generous amount of oil until golden on both sides. Remove with a slotted spatula.
4. Chop coarsely and mix in with tomatoes, garlic, cumin and paprika.
5. Put all this back in the heated frying-pan with a little more oil and cook until dry (about 10 minutes).
6. Place in a bowl to cool. Add lemon juice, salt and pepper to taste.
7. When cool, stir in green herbs or sprinkle them on top.

Serve with lemon wedges.

Matecha M'assala Tomato Jam

Tomato jam is not only found among the many little salads; it is also commonly used with chicken and on harsha bread. Most Moroccan cooks make this by boiling down tomatoes with honey. Paula Wolfert gives a recipe where the tomatoes are scorched in the oven first, which gives the flavour a lot more depth and richness. Tomato jam lasts for a week in the fridge, not that you care, as you will eat it all in one sitting.

Makes approximately 2 cups

2 kg very ripe Roma or acid free tomatoes
2 tbsp extra virgin olive oil
3 tbsp honey – thyme honey is good
1 tsp ground cinnamon
salt and freshly ground pepper to taste
1 tsp orange blossom water
2 tsp sesame seeds

1. Preheat the oven to 250 °C (480 °F) and roast tomatoes whole until they are blackened – takes about half an hour.
2. Once cool, peel, core, deseed and chop. It will be about 4 cups.
3. Heat oil in a medium-sized pot and add chopped tomatoes and any cooking liquid. Cook on a medium heat until completely reduced and very thick – about 10 minutes.
4. Add honey, cinnamon, salt and pepper and cook for another 5 minutes.
5. Remove from the heat and add the orange blossom water.

Serve on a flat plate and sprinkle with sesame seeds.

When David and I mentioned to Adriano that we wanted to treat our gastronomads to a dinner in a private home in the medina, we knew he wouldn't let us down. As Morocco is an interior decorator's paradise, we were looking for a house that would be fabulous as well as having a very good cook. Adriano suggested a togged-up, drop-dead dinner and party at his place around the corner from the hotel. Say 'Party' to a Moroccan and they ask 'Where?'. They would party every night if they could. Far from trying to talk the staff into doing it, they start planning right then and there and bring their friends in to help. And you don't just have a complicated feast with thirty-three hundred dishes but you have live music, dancing, belly dancing and singing.

Adriano's house is very different in decor from the hotel. First of all, it is not a riad; it is a spacious, high, ornate-ceilinged house which was once part of a palace. The first floor houses the salon with a dome, dining room, two bedrooms and a ridiculously small, pokey kitchen from which marvels will emerge. The decor is stylish and restrained. Upstairs there is a two-level terrace and the top of the dome. This is where Adriano and his staff laid out the bar with every kind of wine and cocktail imaginable. The handsome male staff were all kitted out in new uniforms and Amina and the girls were slaving away in their aprons and scarves in the cramped downstairs kitchen. I put my head in and there she was, deep-frying dozens of perfect little briouat triangles stuffed with different things like meat, fish and vegetables.

I had asked her to make one of her specialities that she had cooked for me before – whole chicken with chicken liver sauce. If you mention anything culinary to a Moroccan cook, even in passing, she will remember it and the first opportunity she gets, will cook it for you. This is the nature of Moroccans – their sense of hospitality is deeply ingrained. They never get a thank you or any acknowledgement from Moroccan employers so the excessive gratitude and respect they enjoy from foreigners is most rewarding to them. Also it was my birthday, and I am usually on a plane surrounded by strangers on this day so the fact that Amina was making this dish for me and that I was with friends was such a pleasure. Trying to get this recipe out of Amina was difficult as Moroccan cooks make their dishes differently each time. And then I got an email with the details which didn't even include what to do with the livers but did mention it is a 'special occasion' dish. My research showed that it is probably a Tétouan dish as they make chicken dishes with giblets and livers. Tétouan is a city in the Rif Mountains. It enjoys a very Andalusian-influenced cuisine. I saw Amina cooking her dish in a pot, but the final result appeared roasted and the livers were melting. I saw a woman doing this in Casablanca – she steamed her chicken in a couscousiere then finished it off in the oven. Moroccans often grate onions in recipes which produces a soft, thick sauce.

Chicken with Chicken Liver Sauce

Serves 6

1 large free range or organic chicken
4 cloves garlic, finely chopped
1 tsp ground ginger
1 tsp cumin seeds
1 tsp salt
freshly ground black pepper
1 preserved lemon
2 tbsp smen (rancid butter), butter or olive oil
200 g (½ cup) chicken livers
2 good pinches of saffron, soaked for 15 minutess
   in a little hot water
¾ cup grated onions
2 tbsp each of parsley and coriander, chopped
2 cups water
12 big fat brown olives

1. Dry chickens inside and out and rub with lemon juice and a little salt Pull out excess fat from under skin and around the neck and rump end.
2. Blend together (or you can do it in a mortar and pestle) the garlic, ginger, cumin, salt, pepper, the pulp of the preserved lemon and the butter or oil. Rub this all over, inside and out, the chicken and also the livers.
3. Heat a heavy-based pot and put in chicken, marinade and livers. Add saffron and its water, onion, green herbs and water. Cover and simmer for forty-five minutes, turning chicken every so often.
4. Preheat the oven to 200 °C (390 °F). Remove the chicken and brown in the oven (takes about half an hour). Remove the livers and chop or mash. Pit the olives. Add these back into the sauce along with sliced preserved lemon peel and liver. Reduce sauce until thick – about 15 minutes.

Place chicken on a platter and spoon the sauce over.

Amina also roasted quinces for me, which I adore. Quinces, those apples of Aphrodite, really make me think of the Moorish connection because they are a part of all Mediterranean cuisines. I first tasted baked quince in Portugal – huge, dripping in thick juice and utterly divine. They were halved with skin on and pips in to impart more flavour, then sprinkled with port, sugar, cinnamon, cloves and butter. We all know and love dark golden quince paste – we can hardly imagine a cheese platter without it. I used to flash covetous eyes at my neighbour's quinces until he noticed and gave me some. He smiled when I poached them in Riesling, vincotto, vanilla and saffron and gave them back to him. It is magical to see the hard, pale fruit turn softly red-orange with cooking. If you put a quince in your linen cupboard, everything will smell of their heavenly perfume. Its blossoms are a lovely pink-tinged white. Moorish Prince Ja'far ibn 'Uthman al-Mushafi wrote a famous poem about the erotic symbolism of the quince – its musk-like odour, its nakedness.

A perfume
Penetrating as musk;
Its golden body
Naked in my hand,
Made me think of her I cannot name.
I was breathing so hard
My fingers crushed it.

Cripes!

Amina's favourite thing to cook in the whole world is cakes so we got a selection of three sugary, creamy confections. After dinner the musicians turned up. The staff who don't drink, drank. All hell broke loose. Give a Moroccan a gin and tonic and he's anybody's. They only need one and they start dancing and singing and giving you roses and blowing kisses. I sang a Piaf song, Jeff sang a song and played with the musicians, Jane sang a song, Cassie and Rebecca from Kasbek shimmied with Adriano and even Amina and the girls came in and danced in their dada uniforms. Adriano had the film *Casablanca* screening on one of the walls all night and it would not be gilding the lily to say we were all truly unplugged in Marrakech.

As we hadn't partied quite enough, we rearranged our best clothes and spent our last night at the outrageous and grandiose Dar Yacout restaurant in the medina. We walked into the square and there waiting for us were horse-drawn carriages. It's quite lovely and magical riding in these carriages at night. They are rather wide but somehow manage to squeeze through the narrow medina streets to get to the very hard-to-find destination. The reason you dine at Yacout is so you can pretend to be part of the royal family who dine there from time to time. It is a former palace, completely renovated and redecorated by American architect Bill Wallis over twenty years ago. It used to be the most expensive restaurant in Morocco but that is probably changing now that there is so much money in Marrakech. It is owned by Mohamed Zkhiri and run by his very handsome (another handsome Moroccan) and charming brother. Mohamed has a website which is a sort of online newspaper and very interesting, but there is no website and no email for the restaurant – you have to call to reserve. At the desk they usually pretend they have never heard of you but you ignore that and keep smiling as if you have diamonds in your teeth.

We walk from the muck of the medina into a sparkling, enchanting world, where quite obviously the princesses never wore high heels, as the first thing you do is ascend steep, narrow stairs to the rooftop. On the way I always take the gastronomads into the huge kitchen, full of dadas in white, cooking away either squatting or at a bench or bent over in the common jack-knife position. The decor all over the palace is saturated in beauty with all the traditional tiles, wall finishes, candle light, ornate plaster work and carpets. The rooftop, from which you can gaze over the whole medina and Koutoubia Mosque, while sipping Champagne, is glittering and decorated with sweet-smelling trees and flowers. Built like a giant riad but technically a dar or house, the palace is open to the sky and you can peer down from the roof into the sumptuous dining room below. With a firm grip on the railings, we then descend to the next floor where there are bars, salons and little private rooms for hanging out, North African style. We arrange ourselves in one of these rooms on chairs and sofas, surrounded by luxury, and settle into drinking cocktails. Nothing happens quickly at Yacout – you have to float as in a dream through this process. Musicians are playing everywhere.

Top left: *Grinding argan nuts and then separating out the oil*
Bottom left: *Saffron sorting*
Above: *Adriano and Amina*
Right: *Jane singing*

After a time of wonder, we are led to our table. If it's a good night you sit outside by the dazzling pool; if it's a chilly night you sit inside in one of the many dining rooms. The service by beautifully, traditionally dressed waiters is beyond reproach as they bring in what can only be described as an embarrassment of culinary riches. The meal commences with the now familiar little salad dishes – about fifteen or twenty. This is followed by an assortment of briouats, then chicken tagine, followed by slow-roasted lamb shoulder, followed by lamb and vegetable couscous, followed by a very good milk pastilla, followed by pastries and mint tea. It's all best eaten with the fingers as rose-scented water is passed around. Briouats, in the same family as pastillas, briks and trid, are made by wrapping pastry around other ingredients. Briouats are usually tiny, triangle-shaped, complete flavour explosions. This fragrant briouat recipe was kindly given to me by my Moroccan friend Simo of Simo's restaurant in Christchurch, New Zealand.

Duck and Pear Briouats

1 tbsp olive oil
1 tbsp butter
1 small onion, finely chopped
2 cloves garlic, finely chopped
2 large pears, diced
250 g cooked, shredded duck meat
1 tbsp chopped parsley
1 tbsp chopped coriander
1 tbsp chopped fresh mint
1 tsp cinnamon
1 tsp ground cumin
salt and pepper to taste
1 tbsp honey
1 egg, beaten
filo pastry sheets
1 egg, beaten
100 g clarified butter
50 g sesame seeds

1. In a heavy-based pan, heat oil and butter. Sauté onion and garlic with the pears until golden – about 10 minutes.
2. Add duck meat, herbs, spices and honey and cook together for 5 minutes.
3. Add first measure of beaten egg and stir through the mixture until cooked – about 5 minutes. Set aside to cool.
4. Open filo pastry out and keep covered with a slightly damp tea towel. Cut one sheet into lengthwise strips about 7 cm wide. Place 1 tbsp of the mixture at the bottom of the strips and fold left hand corner over mixture, making a triangle. Fold over and over like a flag, forming a triangle parcel. Seal edge of pastry using second measure of beaten egg. Keep doing this until you have used up all the mixture.
5. Preheat oven to 150 °C (300 °F). Lay briouats in a shallow roasting pan, brush with clarified butter and sprinkle with sesame seeds. Bake for 15 minutes or until golden and crispy.

Eat immediately.

Relaxed by delicious Siroua wine, we come over all sharey and everyone starts saying what they loved about the trip and Marrakech and Yacout and handsome Moroccans and whatever. Honestly, the food is perfectly fine but not quite up to the standard of the location. However, it is absolutely worth going there because Yacout is like nothing else and where else do you get to be a princess for a night?

And so my epicurean sojourn ended, leaving me smelling of rose petals, my feet and hands imprinted with henna swirls and the taste of salty lemons in my mouth. Our culinary week has been a great success, we've gone below the surface and experienced more than just shared food. Strangers who have spent a week together make surprising, life-affirming connections, have cathartic experiences and eat things they never thought they would. I hope they cherish their memories for years to come. As for David, Jeff, Jane and me, we are already dreaming of our next culinary destination, because this is a moveable feast and we can unplug at the drop of a pomegranate.

Image Credits

t: *top*, b: *bottom*, c: *centre*, l: *left*, r: *right*

Cover credits

Gettyimages.co.nz front cover (t, c), back cover
iStockphoto.com front cover (bl, br)
Todd Eyre front cover (image of Peta)

Internal credits

Jane Avery pages 132, 215
Dreamstime.com pages 18, 21, 27, 30, 31, 38, 39, 44, 46–7, 48, 51, 65, 80, 82, 84, 86, 89, 90, 91, 97, 98, 99, 103, 104, 108, 114, 117, 127, 130, 133, 136, 137, 148, 149, 151, 154, 157, 158, 159, 163, 166, 167, 178, 179, 181, 182, 183, 186, 187, 191, 195, 201, 207, 209, 211, 214, 216, 217, 219, 225, 231, 233, 238, 239, 241, 246–7, 252, 253, 255, 257, 259, 265, 268, 269, 270, 271, 277
Gettyimages.co.nz page 3
David Horsman pages 61, 71, 245, 256
iStockphoto.com pages 55, 59, 69, 95, 96, 111, 122, 125, 139, 205, 206, 242–3
Peta Mathias page 75

First colour insert
(between pages 32 and 33)
Jane Avery pages 1, 2, 3 (tr), 5, 6, 8
David Horsman pages 3(b), 7
Peta Mathias pages 3 (tl), 4

Second colour insert
(between pages 64 and 65)
Jane Avery pages 2 (b), 3
David Horsman pages 1, 4 (t, b), 6, 8
Peta Mathias pages 5, 7 (t)
Florence Verley pages 2 (t), 7 (b)

Third colour insert
(between pages 96 and 97)
Jane Avery pages 1, 2 (t), 4 (b), 6 (t), 8
David Horsman pages 2 (b), 3 (t, b), 4 (t), 5, 6 (b), 7

Fourth colour insert
(between pages 112 and 113)
Jane Avery pages 1, 2 (b), 3, 4 (tl, tr, bl), 5, 6–7, 8
David Horsman page 4 (br)
Peta Mathias page 2 (t)

Fifth colour insert
(between pages 160 and 161)
Jane Avery pages 2 (tl), 4 (t)
David Horsman pages 1, 2 (bl, br), 3, 7 (t, b)
Peta Mathias pages 2 (tr), 4 (b), 6 (tr, b)
Adriano Pirani pages 5, 6 (tl), 8

Sixth colour insert
(between pages 208 and 209)
Jane Avery pages 2, 3, 4–5, 6 (t, b), 7, 8
David Horsman page 1

Seventh colour insert
(between pages 240 and 241)
Jane Avery pages 1, 4, 5 (t), 6–7, 8
David Horsman pages 2 (t, b), 3 (t, b)
Peta Mathias page 5 (b)

Eighth colour insert
(between pages 272 and 273)
Jane Avery pages 2 (tl), 5 (b)
David Horsman pages 2 (tr), 3 (t, b), 4 (t, b), 5 (t), 6–7, 8
Peta Mathias pages 1, 2 (b)

General Index

Index Recipes

DVD available through www.petaunplugged.com